AF779493

European Directory of Software for Libraries and Information Centres

European Directory of Software for Libraries and Information Centres

Compiled by Joanna Wood
Library Information Technology Centre, South Bank University

Routledge
Taylor & Francis Group
LONDON AND NEW YORK

First published 1993 by Ashgate Publishing

Reissued 2018 by Routledge
2 Park Square, Milton Park, Abingdon, Oxon OX14 4RN
711 Third Avenue, New York, NY 10017, USA

Routledge is an imprint of the Taylor & Francis Group, an informa business

Copyright © Library Information Technology Centre, South Bank University, London 1993

All rights reserved. No part of this book may be reprinted or reproduced or utilised in any form or by any electronic, mechanical, or other means, now known or hereafter invented, including photocopying and recording, or in any information storage or retrieval system, without permission in writing from the publishers.

Notice:
Product or corporate names may be trademarks or registered trademarks, and are used only for identification and explanation without intent to infringe.

Publisher's Note
The publisher has gone to great lengths to ensure the quality of this reprint but points out that some imperfections in the original copies may be apparent.

Disclaimer
The publisher has made every effort to trace copyright holders and welcomes correspondence from those they have been unable to contact.

A Library of Congress record exists under LC control number : 93171818

ISBN 13: 978-1-138-62441-2 (hbk)
ISBN 13: 978-0-429-46085-2 (ebk)

Contents

Introduction

1. Background

This directory succeeds "A Directory of Library and Information Retrieval Software for Microcomputers" compiled by Hilary Dyer and Alison Gunson which was published most recently by Gower (now Ashgate) in its fourth edition in 1990.

The task of updating this directory was undertaken by the LITC (Library Information Technology Centre) in 1992. The LITC provides information and expertise on library and information software. It publishes books and journals specialising in this area and maintains extensive and up-to-date information on software currently on the market. It is based at South Bank University, London and is partially funded by the British Library Research and Development Department.

Previous editions of the directory have been international, however the majority of packages included were supplied and supported in the UK or US. This directory has a different geographic emphasis aiming to provide a single source of information on microcomputer software for library and information work available and supported in **Europe**. This reflects increased interest in Europe particularly amongst the member states of the European Community, the opening up of Eastern Europe and the desire of most users to purchase software which is supplied and supported locally.

Whilst every effort has been made to make the information contained in this directory as complete as possible, information for some countries was sparse and as a result may not be complete. It is hoped that we will be alerted to any omissions for inclusion in the next edition of the Directory. A database containing the contents of this Directory is being maintained at the LITC and will be kept up-to-date to provide a basis for the next edition.

2. Method

The update to this directory began with analysis of the data collected by Hilary Dyer and Alison Gunson in the form of a database. This was modified to reflect the scope of the new directory, new products were added and existing products updated using resources at the LITC (mainly product literature, journal articles etc) and information supplied by a network of LITC contacts in Europe. Information was stored in two databases, one containing product records and one containing suppliers.

Once information had been collected for as many products as possible, all the suppliers of the products were mailed (or in the case of products with supplier/distributor/dealer networks, the main supplier was mailed). The suppliers were asked to confirm that the details we had were correct, to modify the details if appropriate and to inform us of any other products which they supplied. We had a good response from the suppliers contacted and are grateful to them for their cooperation.

On receipt of replies from suppliers, the databases were duly updated and used to generate the text and indexes for the directory. Data was output in ASCII files with attributes which could be read into Ventura where the text was desk-top published to produce the camera ready copy.

3. Scope

Software has been included in this directory if it comes within each of the following categories :

- **Microcomputer Software**
  It runs on microcomputers supporting MS DOS/PC DOS; OS/2; UNIX; PICK; and APPLE MACINTOSH operating systems. Software running exclusively on BBC microcomputers has not been included.

- **Libraries and Information Centres**
  It is suitable for use in library and information work and particularly if it has one or more of the following functions:
  - Acquisitions
  - Archives
  - Cataloguing
  - CD-ROM interface
  - Circulation
  - Communications
  - Community information
  - Computer aided learning
  - Data entry
  - Data reformatting
  - Free text retrieval
  - Image retrieval
  - Information retrieval
  - Library housekeeping systems

Inter library loans
Media control
Personal bibliographic reference management
Serials control
Thesaurus control
User education
Viewdata

Industry-standard word-processing, spreadsheets, accounts, desk-top publishing or other office administration systems have not been included.

- **Europe**
  It is marketed and supported in any E.E.C. member state together with Scandinavia. This includes Belgium, Denmark, France, Germany, Greece, Eire, Italy, Luxembourg, Netherlands, Portugal, Spain, UK, Sweden, Norway and Finland. For these countries every effort has been made to make the information as complete as possible. Software supplied in other countries has been included where information has been available. However, in these countries no attempt at completeness has been made.

4. How to use this directory

This directory is divided into five sections. The first section is the main section and contains the software entries arranged in alphabetical order by software name. Full details of the suppliers of the software are contained in the second section — the Suppliers Index which is arranged in alphabetical order by supplier name.

Three further indexes are available. The first is a function index using the descriptors listed in the software entries. This is followed by an index according to microcomputer operating systems supported. And finally, a geographic index is included listing products according to the country in which a supplier/dealer/distributor is located.

All the indexes are linked to the software entries section using the software name.

In the software entries section, some products have been identified with an asterisk (*). This indicates that it was not possible to confirm the entries with the suppliers.

5. Content of software entries

Supplier — The software producer if known (includes American companies for reference purposes)

European Dealers/Distributors — Names of any Europe-based companies known to be marketing and supporting the software

General Details — Brief information about the software

Descriptors

Operating System — Normally microcomputer operating systems. The software may also run on other operating systems — this should be confirmed with the supplier concerned

Special Hardware Requirements

Price Range — Price bands (A-E) have been used to give an indication of the price of the software. These provide a rough guide only. Accurate pricing of software should always be obtained from suppliers direct as prices can vary according to the application of the individual purchaser.

A rough guide to the price bands used in the software entries is given below in a variety of currencies. The rates are based on those quoted on 15 September 1992.

Country/Currency	A	B	C	D	E
UK	<500	500-1000	1000-5000	5000-10000	10000+
FRANCE	<4625	4625-9250	9250-46250	46250-92500	92500+
GERMANY	<1370	1370-2740	2740-13700	13700-27400	27400+
ITALY	<1087500	1087500-2175000	2175000-10875K	10875K-21750K	21750K+
SPAIN	<87500	87500-175000	175000-875000	875000-1750000	1750000+
SWITZERLAND	<1210	1210-2420	2420-12100	12100-24200	24200+
GREECE	<167500	167500-335000	335000-1675000	1675000-3350000	3350000+
DENMARK	<5285	5285-10570	10570-52850	52850-105700	105700+
NORWAY	<5425	5425-10850	10850-54250	54250-108500	108500+
SWEDEN	<5040	5040-10080	10080-50400	50400-100800	100800+
NETHERLANDS	<1545	1545-3090	3090-15450	15450-30900	30900+
BELGIUM	<28100	28100-56200	56200-281000	281000-562000	562000+

Languages — Spoken languages in which the software and documentation is available

Reviews — References to relevant articles in the literature

Please note that information contained in the records was compiled from product literature and other published material or has been written by the suppliers themselves. The contents of the records do not therefore represent any form of recommendation. Where records vary in length, this reflects the amount of information available and not any tacit recommendation on the part of the LITC. For some products we were unable to obtain any more details than the supplier's name and address. These products have nevertheless been included to provide as complete a listing as possible.

6. Acknowledgements

My grateful thanks to all those who helped in the compilation of this directory. In particular to Hilary Dyer and Alison Gunson compilers of the fourth edition; to Caroline Moore and Rosemary Russell and the staff of the LITC for their help, patience and support; to Louise Manners for all her typing work; to Katrina Bloxham for producing the camera-ready copy.

Thanks to all those who provided information on European products including Pat Manson, DG XIIIB, Luxembourg; John Baker; John Aanonson, UKOLUG; VOGIN; Antti Soini, Automation Unit of Finnish Research Libraries; J Van Borm, the University of Antwerp; Alice Keefer, Doc 6; Gitte Larsen, Royal School of Librarianship, Denmark; Lucy Tedd, Editor, Program; Dr Louis Lee, University of Westminster. Thank you also to all suppliers who sent in up-to-date information without which the directory could not have been produced.

Finally thank you to my husband, Martin and my family for their unfailing support throughout the project.

Joanna Wood
LITC
September 1992

Software Entries

ABEKT *

Supplier — National Documentation Centre (Greece)

General Details — Abekt is a cataloguing and enquiry system for IBM PCs and compatibles running in monochrome only. The catalogue structure is fixed and fields are standard on the system making it best-suited to monograph and series material. A separate module provides authority control enabling the user to prepare lists and print lists of preferred terms. These lists, however, cannot be displayed during data entry. Searching is by keyword, personal name and the abbreviated forms of corporate source, title, publisher, series, ISBN and unique number. Boolean combinations can be carried out on previously created sets using a function key to select the appropriate operator. There is a choice of 2 formats of records for display and printing out. While there is some screen prompting, users need to be familiar with the system to use it successfully. There are no help screens. Screen displays are in Greek, however data can be entered in Greek or Latin character sets if supported by the hardware.

Descriptors — Cataloguing; Information retrieval

Operating System — MS DOS

Languages — Greek

ABSYS *

Supplier — Servicios De Teledocumentacion, S.A.; Eurotelematica

General Details — ABSYS is a library housekeeping system which was developed by integrating BRS/Search (see BRS/Search) with the relational database: INFORMIX 4GL, thereby offering both powerful searching and good relational facilities. The system is comprehensive with modules for acquisitions (including budget control), cataloguing (supporting MARC formats), serials control, circulation control and an online public access catalogue.

Descriptors — Integrated library housekeeping system; Acquisitions; Cataloguing; Circulation; Serials control; OPAC

Operating System — UNIX

Special Hardware Requirements — 4 Mbytes RAM; 25 Mbytes of main memory

Price Range — Depends on size of installation

Languages — Spanish; Catalan; French; English

ACOM

European Dealers/Distributors — Information Automation Ltd (UK)

General Details — ACOM is a communications package with many powerful and flexible features specifically tailored to the online handling, uploading and downloading needs of online searchers. The full package provides both communications features and search assistance on a range of hosts. A memory resident version (ACOM-MR) provides search assistance as a pop-up option over a user's existing communications software. A unique feature is the automatic translation between the different command languages used by eight popular hosts. While online, searchers have access to many different standard features as well as some rather more unusual ones such as the ability to recall and edit the last line transmitted, or to clear the current line to allow it to be retyped before transmitting, and calling up customised help information. A stop watch display gives automatic tracking of the elapsed time since running ACOM. In addition to these features which apply to any host searched using ACOM, for specific hosts (currently BRS, Data-Star, Dialog, ESA, FizTechnik, Mead Data, ORBIT and Telesystemes), there are two additional features: Userguides and the translation option. The Userguides contain database and command information specific to that service, and can be loaded as required. The translation feature enables users to search any of the supported hosts using whichever of the search languages they prefer, and can operate automatically or under the user's control. Function keys control access to Userguide screens, to the ACOM-MR main menu, and also the use of the translation feature. There is also an upload feature based on stored searches from which lines can be selected for sending to the host. Translation can operate with these lines if required.

Descriptors — Communications; Downloading; Online search aid

Operating System — MS DOS

Price Range — A

Languages — English

Reviews — ACOM and ACOM-MR: the software that online searchers have been waiting for? *Library Micromation News*, 33, September 1991.

ADIOS *

Supplier — Synaps Automatisering bv

General Details — A cataloguing and library administration system.

Descriptors — Cataloguing

Operating System — MS DOS; UNIX

ADLIB LITE

Supplier — Databasix Information Systems bv; Adlib Information Systems Ltd

General Details — ADLIB Lite is a PC-based version of the ADLIB Library and Collection management system. It was launched in 1992 with cataloguing and circulation modules and further housekeeping functions are planned for the future. The software contains a standard library model system that enables users to run the system immediately after installation, while allowing modifications to meet specific user requirements. The system is menu-driven with context-specific help which can be modified by the user. It incorporates a user-defined range of indexes that ensure fast access to the database and also provides free text index facilities that include lists of all relevant words, phrases, terms etc used in the database. ADLIB Lite is multilingual in its approach and can be run simultaneously in any language including English, Dutch and French.

Descriptors — Integrated library housekeeping system; Cataloguing; Circulation; OPAC

Operating System — MS DOS

Price Range — B (Single user); C (Multi user)

Languages — English; Dutch; French

AFIBYBLOS *

Supplier — Agence Française Informatique

General Details — Afibyblos is a real-time library management system providing acquisitions, cataloguing and retrieval, serials control, circulation and inter-library loans. The cataloguing module is suitable for multi-media applications, meets ISBD standards and is compatible with UNIMARC. Authority control is available and the thesaurus can be viewed and modified via windows over the cataloguing screen. There are two levels of search: a simple search for end-users incorporating use of the AND or OR Boolean operators; and a more sophisticated search level for professionals where Boolean operators can be used for all fields within the catalogue.

Descriptors — Integrated library housekeeping system; Cataloguing ; Acquisitions; Circulation; Serials control; Inter-library loans

Operating System — MS DOS; OS/2

Price Range — C

Languages — French

AIM-2

Supplier — De Montfort University Library

General Details — An inter-library loans package designed to administer borrowing and lending between the user library and British Library Document Supply Centre or any other loans facility. The system also covers: management information; security procedures; print facilities and communications. AIM is available in two versions. The standard version is available from Dawson Technology and has been incorporated into the OASIS product range (see OASIS-AIM and OASIS). De Montfort University supply a version in which the underlying software (DELTA) can be modified by the user allowing the system to be customised.

Descriptors — Inter-library loans

Operating System — MS DOS

Price Range — C

Languages — English

Reviews — Leeves, J., *A guide to inter-library loan management systems.* LINC, 1991. Marks, C., Inter-library lending packages: a review. *Library Micromation News*, 28, June 1990.

ALEPH/PC

European Dealers/Distributors — Ex Libris S.A. (World-wide distributor); Data Koncept (Denmark); IBR (Hungary); Deinfor S.A. (Spain)

General Details — Aleph is a comprehensive modular integrated library housekeeping system consisting of 6 real-time modules: cataloguing and holdings, search (OPAC), authority control, circulation, serials control, acquisitions; and 3 batch-mode modules: library utilities, import and export, and management. The system can operate in a range of languages which can be defined by the user for all screens, error messages etc. it can also handle multiscript data, presently Latin, Greek, Cyrillic, Hebrew and Arabic. Cataloguing is MARC compatible and full-screen editing is available. A thesaurus is built automatically as part of the cataloguing process for the author, title and subject fields. Searching is flexible with Boolean operators to refine searches, a command-driven option (using the CCL — Common Command Language) for more complex requirements and up to 99 different user-defined display formats. The circulation module provides the functions of issue, return, renewal and reservations and allows the library to define its own parameters for the control of loans. Acquisitions is fully integrated into the catalogue and incorporates invoice processing and budgetary control.

The serials control module automates check-in, maintains a serials holdings file, generates routing slips and monitors binding requirements.

Descriptors — Integrated library housekeeping system; Cataloguing; Circulation; Acquisitions; Serials control; Thesaurus control

Operating System — MS DOS; OS/2; UNIX

Price Range — D/E

Languages — Spanish; English; Danish; Hungarian; Italian; German; French; Hebrew

ALEXANDRIE II *

Supplier — Gestion Business Concept

General Details — Alexandrie permits the storage of all types of document (books, journals, audio-visual material, plans etc). Retrieval is available using a variety of criteria combined using Boolean operators (AND, OR, NOT). Search strategies can be stored for re-use. A thesaurus facility is present together with a loans management option.

Descriptors — Information retrieval; Circulation; Thesaurus control

Operating System — APPLE OPERATING SYSTEM

Price Range — C

Languages — French

ALICE *

Supplier — Softlink Europe Ltd

General Details — Alice forms one of a suite of programs for school administration and is used in school libraries and resource centres as well as in special libraries. The program is written in C and Clipper and provides for all the functions of the library: library management, circulation, user enquiry (OPAC), acquisitions, periodicals, communications, remote access, report generator and union catalogue. Data is entered in the library management module in a set of standard fields of which the author, publisher, subject and series fields are authority controlled. The circulation module includes standard loans functions but in addition provides for bookings and grouping of items together into 'resource boxes' to be loaned as a single unit — suitable for the loan of class sets. The OPAC is a simple catalogue enquiry to be used by end-users and staff, and users from other sites can also access the catalogue using the remote access function. The system is fully integrated but can be bought on a modular basis if required. A multi-user version is available which can run on any network which supports DOS 3.1 record locking.

Descriptors — Integrated library housekeeping system; Cataloguing; OPAC; Circulation; Acquisitions; Serials control

Operating System — MS DOS

Price Range — C

Languages — English

Reviews — Baker, J., Of wonderland and headless chickens.... *VINE*, 87, June 1992.

AMITEL

Supplier — Robert Fox and Associates

European Dealers/Distributors — Informed Business Services

General Details — Amitel has been designed to take account of the problems encountered by many business users of dial-up remote online databases. It aims to provide an easy-to-use, yet powerful, package. Its most unusual feature is providing access to Minitel, the French viewdata system, the Danish viewdata system (with a Danish character set option) and also to British viewdata systems and to all teletype systems (Datastar, Dialog, ESA, PFDS, FT Profile, etc.). It also provides VT100 terminal emulation. Amitel is easy-to-use, with well laid out screens, good use of colour and helpful prompts throughout. Once online, users of viewdata systems should find most features they require are supported including data downloading and page store facilities. However, when online in teletype mode, experienced searchers may find the features are somewhat limited — in particular no uploading facilities exist.

Descriptors — Communications; Viewdata

Operating System — MS DOS

Price Range — A

Languages — English

Reviews — Amitel and Communicator: two new communications packages for online searchers. *Library Micromation News*, 31, March 1991.

ANALOGIO *

Supplier — Comsys (Greece)

General Details — Analogio is a library housekeeping system based on Clipper with C language enhancements. It comes as a complete system and provides the functions of acquisitions (orders and suppliers), cataloguing and a users database for handling loans. Integration of the system is limited. Cataloguing is based on a fixed structure geared to monographs. Authors and subjects are authority controlled. Records are held at the title level and all records have to be entered from the keyboard as it is not possible to import data. Searching facilities are basic and the Boolean AND is available for combining name and subject searches. Within circulation the functions of issues, returns, overdues and reservations are available.

Descriptors — Integrated library housekeeping system; Cataloguing; Circulation

Operating System — MS DOS

Languages — Greek

ARTEMIS

Supplier — Imago Logica

General Details — Artemis is a library database management system with facilities for lending administration, cataloguing, ordering administration, searching using a list of synonyms and phonetic searching.

Descriptors — Cataloguing; Circulation; Acquisitions

Operating System — MS DOS

Price Range — C

Languages — Dutch; English

ASCOM IV

European Dealers/Distributors — Telesystems Ltd

General Details — ASCOM is a general-purpose communications package offering a wide variety of terminal emulations. Terminals emulated include DEC VT 100, DEC VT 52, ADDS, Viewpoint, Televideo 912, IBM 3101, LSI ADM3A, Hazeltine 1500. There are more than 60 commands and a built-in editor.

Descriptors — Communications

Operating System — MS DOS

Price Range — A

Languages — English

ASKSAM *

European Dealers/Distributors — North American Software GmbH (Germany); Stichting Vrienden van Archief en Librije (Netherlands)

General Details — AskSam is an information storage and retrieval system designed to operate in the IBM PC and compatible environment, for use with both text and numeric information. Files consist of records that may contain free form text and/or variable length fields. Records can be linked to form unlimited length documents. Records may be updated at any time with a full screen text editor. It is possible to retrieve and sort on anything entered in a record, including a single character, wild cards, calendar dates and arithmetic comparisons. Multiple records may be updated using batch operations. Other features include: word processing capabilities and a command language; the creating and use of stored programs; passwords and encryption; proximity searching; a report generator; automatic phone dialler; hypertext facility; online context sensitive help, and an optional index facility; global scanning; dialogue boxes; shell to DOS; linkage of graphic images to text files, and the ability to spawn templates and program records to a new file. Output may be routed to the screen, printer or disk, and the import or export of ASCII files from other systems, including dBase, is supported. Applications available include bibliographic reports, inventories, and book ordering systems. A network version is available. Educational pricing is offered.

Descriptors — Hypertext; Information retrieval

Operating System — MS DOS

Price Range — A

Languages — English

Reviews — Côté, R. and Diehl, S., Searching for common threads. *BYTE*, June 1992.
askSam, Version 4.2. *PC Magazine*, September 1989, pp.54, 56.
Brown, B., Personal information managers:askSam. (One of 33 product evaluations included in *PC Magazine*'s The Best of 1988). *PC Magazine*, 8 (1), January 1989, 139(2).
Emmerson, B., askSam. *Which Computer (UK)*, July 1989, 87 - 8.
Grevstad, E., AskSam 4.1; outstanding, in or out of its fields. *PC Resource*, April 1989, 132 - 134.
Grunin, L., A 75 dollar runtime version of askSam. *PC Magazine*, January 1989, 54.

Kittle, W., AskSam for your data! A look at text-based management. *Database*, 12 (1), 99-101.
Marks, K., ASKSAM: an on-line personnel system. In *Computers in Libraries 1989. 4th annual conference and exhibition. Conference proceedings.* Meckler, 91 - 93.
Name, M.L. Van and Catchings, B., HyperSift; the ticket to askSam. *PC Computing*, 2 (3), March 1989, 39 (2).
Rupley, S., Capen, T., and Richey, J., Quiet please, text search in progress; six text databases that comb the stacks for missing text. *InfoWorld*, 11 (44), October 1989, 55 (12).
Veccia, S., Software pick of the month: AskSam. *Database*, 12 (2), 128.
AskSam zoeken zonder samenhang. *PC Active*, 30, 1991, 6 - 7.

ASSASSIN PC

Supplier — Associated Knowledge Systems

General Details — This is the PC version of Assassin. The software permits the storage and retrieval of free form text. Data entry features include prompted direct screen input, and a word processing interface. Items may be allocated to one of nine files and can be classified as confidential for security purposes. Personal names, words and phrases may be indexed. Full text and marked word indexing are possible within a single item. Search facilities include automatic synonym searches, nested Boolean logic, and search limitation by files or dates. There is a string search feature for words not indexed, and full or part display of selected items. Print facilities are available, and output may be to disk for incorporation into other documents. The system features online index maintenance including synonyms. The system has both "novice" and "expert" modes, and a "help" facility.

Descriptors — Information retrieval

Operating System — MS DOS

Price Range — B

Languages — English

Reviews — Clough, R., ASSASSIN: the ongoing development of a text storage and retrieval system. *Information Services & Use*, 9, 1989, 140 - 160.

ATBIB

Supplier — ATBiB bv

General Details — ATBiB is an integrated cataloguing and loans program. It is menu-driven and user-friendly making it suitable for both end-users and professionals. The system is suitable for multi-media requirements including books, theses, serials, videos, software etc. Most of the fields can be searched and Boolean operators can be used to combine terms and fields.

Descriptors — Cataloguing; Information retrieval; Circulation

Operating System — MS DOS

Special Hardware Requirements — Minimum configuration 286-based PC; 386-based PC preferable.

Price Range — B (basic module)

Languages — Dutch; French; English (under development)

ATHENE *

Supplier — Southdata Ltd

General Details — Athene is a low-cost document-imaging and text retrieval system combining: Alex advanced Optical Character Recognition system and Colossus high speed, text oriented database manager. Alex automatically reads all the typed and printed words in a document; Colossus uses these words to index the image of the document, so that the user can retrieve it by searching on anything in it. The user can then type in comments on the document which are stored directly in the Colossus database and are instantly available to all users of the system. (See also Colossus and Superfile).

Descriptors — Information retrieval; Image processing

Operating System — MS DOS

Languages — English

AUTOBIBLIO

Supplier — BIOSOFT

General Details — AutoBiblio (Version 2.0) stores references and enables their selection, recall and printing in the format required by any journal. It is designed to allow users to create their own database of literature references and to automatically incorporate those cited in papers into their bibliography listings. There are three modules: MakeBiblio, EditRefs and ReadDB. The former searches the manuscript disk and prepares alphabetised or number-order lists of references which it finds cited in the text. It can read Text and ASCII files and also text prepared with Microsoft Word. MakeBiblio also prepares the final bibliography in the format required by any chosen journal. EditRefs prepares the database of references. Records include bibliographic details and abstracts of up to 50 lines and up to 10,000 records can be stored. Searching facilities include field-specific searching, string searching, word adjacency, re-use of search sets and index browsing. The ReadDB module can read information from virtually any database, including Medline, Current Contents and BRS, or from users' previous papers.

Descriptors — Information retrieval; Personal bibliographic database; Reference management

Operating System — APPLE OPERATING SYSTEM

Price Range — A

Languages — English

BABYLONE DOCUMENTATION *

Supplier — Anthesis

General Details — Babylone Documentation permits the storage and retrieval of structured information. It features descriptive data entry using a user-definable format; the construction of a thesaurus; retrieval of records entered; display, printing and exporting of records stored using user-defined formats; loans of books and periodicals etc.

Descriptors — Information retrieval; Circulation

Operating System — APPLE OPERATING SYSTEM

Price Range — C

Languages — French

BASIL *

Supplier — Cristad

General Details — The Basil software for communications comprises 5 main programs accessed through a menu using natural language dialogue. The system offers an online help program, a connection procedures recording program, an intelligent text editor with line by line syntax analysis enabling the construction of search strategies. A further program is available for executing and modifying the strategy, recording the online session, and connection charge accounting. A fifth program enables the reformatting, sorting, paging and printing of search results.

Descriptors — Communications; Online search aid

Operating System — MS DOS

Languages — French

BIB/SEARCH

European Dealers/Distributors — Information Automation Ltd (UK); EPMS bv (European Distribution)

General Details — BiB/SEARCH is an extremely fast and powerful self-contained bibliographic text retrieval and maintenance package which automatically translates downloaded data from DIALOG, BRS, etc. into BiB format. It also has a report generator with menu selectable bibliographic styles. Manual data input has index assisted validation. Searching is fast and includes within phrase truncation and field searching. Online help, manual and command demonstrations are available.

Descriptors — Personal Bibliographic Database; Downloading; Reference management; Data reformatting; Information retrieval

Operating System — MS DOS; UNIX

Price Range — B

Languages — English; Dutch; French; Italian

Reviews — Saari, D.S., A first look at BiB/Search bibliographic database management system. *Database*, 12 (3), 67 - 69.
Perez, E., BiB/Search for text and structured databases. *Online Review*, 12 (4), 219 - 223.
Hanson, T., Managing personal files. *Times Higher Education Supplement*, 15 June 1990.
Hanson, T., BiB/Search. *Library Micromation News*, 27, March 1990.

BIB/TRANS *

European Dealers/Distributors — EPMS bv (Netherlands)

General Details — BiB/TRANS is a data reformatting package for microcomputers.

Descriptors — Data reformatting

Operating System — MS DOS

Price Range — A

BIBAL *

Supplier — LOGi +

General Details — Bibal is a library housekeeping system providing acquisitions, cataloguing and retrieval, serials control, circulation control using barcodes and a Minitel option for remote searching and reservations. Searching facilities include right- and left-hand truncation and Boolean and range operators. A thesaurus option is currently under development.

Descriptors — Integrated library housekeeping system; Acquisitions; Cataloguing; Serials control; Circulation

Operating System — MS DOS

Price Range — B/C

Languages — French

BIBIS

Supplier — Square bv

General Details — BIBIS is an integrated library housekeeping system offering real-time updating, multi-tasking and user-friendly screens. It has modules for cataloguing, purchase order administration, acquisitions list, loan administration and periodical circulation. The catalogue is based on a catalogue card record with an attached free text abstract. A variety of searching approaches are offered including use of Boolean operators. BIBIS can produce printed reports using different layouts and a document generator is available to allow users to define their own layouts. The cataloguing module also incorporates a thesaurus. Order administration, claiming and historical orders are available within the purchase order module. The loans module manages loans, returns, reservations, overdues and statistics and can accommodate the use of barcodes.

Descriptors — Integrated library housekeeping system; Cataloguing; Acquisitions; Circulation; Serials control; Thesaurus control

Operating System — MS DOS; UNIX; VMS

Languages — Dutch; English

BIBLIO *

Supplier — SWS SoftWare Systems AG

General Details — No details supplied for this software package.

BIBLIO-LINK *

Supplier — Personal Bibliographic Software

General Details — Biblio-Link is a set of companion programs to Pro-Cite. It converts records downloaded from an online database into a format acceptable to Pro-Cite. The various bibliographic elements, such as author, title, and publication date, are transferred into the appropriate fields according to document type. The downloaded records can then be merged with existing, manually entered records or stored in a separate Pro-Cite database. The Biblio-Link programs work with downloaded references from hosts such as DIALOG and STN which are processed through the Biblio-Links into a Pro-Cite database. Input may also come from various CD-ROM products such as DIALOG's Medline Ondisk. The new release of the BRS Biblio-Link can now be used with ORBIT and Datastar online services. (See also Pro-Cite).

Descriptors — Data reformatting

Operating System — MS DOS; APPLE OPERATING SYSTEM

Price Range — A

Languages — English

Reviews — Hanson, T.A. and Hanson, A.C., Managing bibliographies with Pro-Cite.

Aslib Proceedings, 41 (2), February 1989, 75 - 83.
Hanson, T., Pro-Cite and Bibliolinks. *Library Micromation News* 26, December 1989.
Joy, A.H., Using PBS' Biblio-Link programs for international/special databases. In *Computers in Libraries 1989*. 4th annual conference & exhibition. *Conference proceedings*. Meckler, 75 - 77.
Joy, A.H., Using PBS' Biblio-Link programs for international special databases. *Library Software Review*, 8 (6), 1989, 341 - 342.

BIBLIO-PLUS

Supplier — Cart Systems

General Details — Biblio-Plus is an easy to use library cataloguing, circulation and retrieval system for the professional and the novice user. Retrieval can be done by title, author, key description etc on a free query basis. Borrower administration and reporting facilities are also available. The system makes use of intuitive functions, on-line help, pop-up menus and single keystroke commands to provide a simple system requiring little training. Networking is possible using network software such as Novell.

Descriptors — Cataloguing; Circulation

Operating System — MS DOS

Price Range — A

Languages — Dutch; English

BIBLIO-TECH *

Supplier — Platinum S.A.

European Dealers/Distributors — Servicios Auxiliares Linguisticos (Spain)

General Details — Library management software developed on 4th dimension, a relational database. Manages books, articles and magazines with flexible record layout with descriptive text of up to 32,000 characters and good retrieval. The cataloguing module includes thesaurus control and a videotext interface is available.

Descriptors — Integrated library housekeeping system; Thesaurus control; Cataloguing; Information retrieval; Acquisitions; Circulation

Operating System — APPLE OPERATING SYSTEM

Languages — English; French

BIBLIOMAC

Supplier — Micro Consulting S.A.

European Dealers/Distributors — Bibliotheks Centrum Sverige AB (BiC)

General Details — BiblioMac is an integrated system for libraries and documentation centres. Its main functions include: cataloguing, using ISBD rules, of any kind of documents (monographs, articles, periodicals, non-book material); retrieval and OPAC; address file management; loan management; loan statistics; issues control. The system is written using 4th Dimension, a relational database package and is made up from a series of interlinked files. It is easy-to-use using the Mac interface to full effect and is available in both single- and multi-user versions.

Descriptors — Cataloguing; Information retrieval; OPAC; Circulation; Serials control

Operating System — APPLE OPERATING SYSTEM

Special Hardware Requirements — Macintosh range of computers with at least 4 Mb of RAM. Supplier's recommended hardware: Mac II, IIsi, IIcx, IIci, IIfx.

Price Range — C

Languages — English; French; German; Swedish (available 1993)

Reviews — BiblioMac — Library software for the Apple Macintosh. *VINE*, 79, August 1990.

BIBLIOMATIK *

Supplier — DANTEK

General Details — No details supplied for this software package.

BIBLION

Supplier — Nivoo

General Details — Biblion is a computer program designed to store, edit, select and print bibliographic information. It can be described as a multi-entrance card-box storing information about books, journals and other publications. There are 17 standard fields including author(s), editor, title, edition, publisher, place and date of publication, keyword, abstract etc. Each card-box can contain up to 99,999 records.

Descriptors — Information retrieval; Personal bibliographic database; Reference management

Operating System — MS DOS

Price Range — A

Languages — Dutch; German; English (under development)

BIBLIOTHEEK EN DOCUMENTATIE PAKKET (BGD - PAKKET) *

Supplier — Ormas Automatisering

General Details — A cataloguing and library administration system.

Descriptors — Cataloguing

Operating System — MS DOS; UNIX

BIBLIX *

European Dealers/Distributors — Borgeaud Informatique

General Details — Biblix is a library housekeeping system with modules covering cataloguing, serials control, circulation and statistics. Biblix has its own internal cataloguing format but can exchange data in Opsys and UNIMARC formats amongst others. Searching is possible over a wide range of fields and a variety of report formats — standard or user-definable are available.

Descriptors — Integrated library housekeeping system; Cataloguing; Serials control; Circulation

Operating System — MS DOS

Price Range — C/D

Languages — French

BIBULUS *

Supplier — TITE-LIVE S.A.

General Details — No details supplied for this software package.

BIDO *

Supplier — Hilberink Computertechniek

General Details — A cataloguing and library administration system.

Descriptors — Cataloguing

Operating System — MS DOS; UNIX

BIDOC *

Supplier — Forrez

General Details — No details supplied for this software package.

BIFAC *

Supplier — BHS

General Details — Bifac is an information retrieval system. It includes a thesaurus and flexible searching on a variety of fields using a variety of search criteria. It also incorporates circulation functions with statistics.

Descriptors — Information retrieval; Thesaurus control

Operating System — MS DOS

Price Range — B/C

Languages — French

BIS-LOK *

Supplier — DABIS-Gesellschaft für Datenbank-Informations systeme mbH

European Dealers/Distributors — DABIS (Austria)

General Details — DABIS has developed BIS-LOK for small and medium-sized libraries working autonomously, while also catering for cooperative libraries. It is based on the BIS system which runs on mainframes. It was developed in cooperation with major university libraries. Its modular basis allows continued development. It is written in C and has variable field lengths and windowing. A network version is available.

Descriptors — OPAC; Cataloguing; Acquisitions; Circulation; Serials control; Integrated library housekeeping system

Operating System — MS DOS; UNIX

Price Range — C

Languages — German; Spanish; Hungarian

BLACKWELL'S CONNECT

Supplier — B.H. Blackwell Ltd (Periodicals Division)

General Details — Blackwell's Connect is an on-line order, enquiry, claiming and messaging link to B.H. Blackwell Ltd.

Descriptors — Acquisitions; Online ordering

Operating System — MS DOS

Price Range — A

Languages — English

BLAISE RECORDER

Supplier — The British Library National Bibliographic Service

General Details — BLAISE Recorder is a communications package and was launched by the British Library in 1987. It can be used to connect to any online service supporting teletype access, but it has been designed primarily for use with BLAISE RECORDS (the British Library's record supply service) and has some particular features suited to this. BLAISE Recorder provides facilities for storing logon parameters for one host; automatic logging on (this is limited as the package does not support auto dial modems, nor does it permit complete host profiles to be set up); uploading by block and flexible downloading. An interesting feature is a recycling program which can be used online to edit automatically stored searches by removing requests which have been satisfied and allowing only the remainder to be matched against other databases.

Descriptors — Communications; Online search aid; Downloading

Operating System — MS DOS

Price Range — A

Languages — English

Reviews — Moore, C., BLAISE Recorder: communications software for information retrieval and record supply. *VINE*, 71, October 1989, 18 - 24.

BLUEBERRY *

European Dealers/Distributors — EPMS bv

General Details — Blueberry is a data reformatting package for microcomputers.

Descriptors — Data reformatting

Operating System — MS DOS

Price Range — A

BOOKMARC

Supplier — LIBPAC Computer Systems Ltd

General Details — BookMarc is a cataloguing system with a window-based interface and MARC compatibility. Its features include full screen text entry and editing, automatic copying of data from authority files and thesaurus file access for the standardisation of terms. An OPAC is available with comprehensive searching facilities. Printed catalogue production and microfiche production are supported and data can be imported and exported in MARC format.

Descriptors — Cataloguing

Operating System — MS DOS

Price Range — C

Languages — English

BREAKOUT PLUS *

Supplier — PC Communications Ltd

General Details — Breakout Plus is a communications program/modem package. Breakout Plus's overlapping menu system has been designed to enable a new user to get the feel of the system very quickly. The menus always show which path has been taken to reach a particular option, showing precisely how the software is structured. Breakout Plus can dial an "unknown" telephone number, check that another communications system is present at the remote end and automatically set the PC with all the correct parameters for instant communications. These vital parameters (parity, echo, data rate and terminal type) as well as telephone number, remote computer name and passwords are stored on individually named mastercards within Breakout Plus. Once a mastercard has been set up, calls can be made simply by selecting the appropriate mastercard from the mastercard list. On most occasions a user dialling into a remote computer will be prompted for identification numbers and passwords. Breakout Plus's is able to automate the appropriate responses. Each individual mastercard allows a logon sequence to be set up which enables pre-defined information to be processed efficiently without manual intervention. Autologon can also be used to automate regular collection of information from a remote computer. Breakout Plus enables a PC to act as a Viewdata (40 and 80 column), Teletype, VT100 or VT52 terminal with more capabilities than an equivalent stand-alone terminal. It automatically recognises which type of display card (VGA, EGA, MCGA, CGA, Hercules or monochrome) a PC is fitted with and adjusts graphic displays accordingly.

Descriptors — Communications; Online search aid; Viewdata

Operating System — MS DOS

Price Range — A/B/C depending on the type of modem.

Languages — English

BRS/SEARCH

Supplier — BRS Software Products Europe; BRS Software Products Benelux; BRS Software Products Scandinavia A/S

European Dealers/Distributors — SINORG (France); IOTA Consultancy (Netherlands)

General Details — BRS/Search is a powerful text retrieval system, able to handle both structured and unstructured text equally well. Using the many configuration options, BRS/Search can be tailored to many different requirements. A "file layout" may be created for each database on a "database design form", enabling data to be formatted according to user requirements. BRS/Search permits a maximum of 16 million documents per database, 65,000 paragraphs per document, 225 sentences per paragraph and 255 words per sentence. Online updating is possible. Databases are searched in natural language, and Boolean, positional and nested searching are possible. There is also a root command to display terms beginning with a specific word stem. The system offers right-hand, left-hand and embedded truncation, and range searching on numbers. Search strategies can be stored and used at a later time. BRS Searchmate has been developed as a menu-driven interface and BRS Maint provides menu-driven control of database creation, maintenance and other system-wide features. Two additional features are: print-time formatting which enables the user to define the format of the text as it is displayed and printed as well as producing formatted reports; and MNS, a high level language which enables users to design their own interface. Optional add-ons are: DEMON - a screen editor developed to control and guide the creation of a document to be loaded into BRS/Search; BRS/Thesaurus — full capability to develop a controlled vocabulary e.g. broader term, narrower term, synonym. It conforms to the international standard ANSI Z.39 plus extensions. A number of new features are available with release 6.0 including database concatenation, automatic searching of plurals, ranked display of documents, external sort facility, hyperlinks and graphical user interfaces running under MS-WINDOWS and X-WINDOWS.

Descriptors — Information retrieval; Thesaurus control

Operating System — UNIX; MS DOS; MS WINDOWS; VAX/VMS

Price Range — C/D/E

Languages — English; Contact local dealer for details of other language versions available

Reviews — Bain, M. and others, *Free text retrieval systems: a review and evaluation.* London: Taylor Graham, 1989.

CAIRS IMS *

Supplier — CAIRS Information Systems

European Dealers/Distributors — IDE (Netherlands)

General Details — CAIRS IMS is one of the longest established packages in the information retrieval market in the UK. It is best suited to structured text and can provide up to 5 separate databases each with its own structure and retrieval requirements. Within each database, size is limited only by the hardware, although there are limits of 99 fields per record and 10,000 characters per field. Records can span up to nine formatted data entry screens. Interactive editing facilities can recall any screen and change all or part of any field. Indexing terms may be taken from the data fields or added manually. There is an optional thesaurus which can be used on data entry and retrieval to create a list of "go" and "stop" words and to establish relationships between words. Search facilities include features such as Boolean logic, truncation, set creation and refinement, and text scanning of unindexed data. There are 26 output formats and the possibility of adding security restrictions. Bulletin production and current awareness searching are possible. In addition, there are printed index and catalogue generation facilities. A network version of CAIRS IMS is available.

Descriptors — Information retrieval; Thesaurus control

Operating System — MS DOS; UNIX; OS/2; A variety of other operating systems

Price Range — B/C/D

Languages — English

CAIRS LMS *

Supplier — CAIRS Information Systems

European Dealers/Distributors — IDE (Netherlands)

General Details — CAIRS LMS is an integrated library housekeeping system derived from Leatherhead Food R.A.'s information retrieval system (see CAIRS IMS). It is particularly popular in special libraries with its emphasis on good retrieval and reporting capabilities. The system is both menu-driven and command-driven, the latter providing very fast access to its facilities for experienced users. CAIRS LMS comes as a pre-defined library application, however, it is possible to obtain the database design module which allows the user to customise the library databases to meet the library's specific needs. CAIRS LMS is based on the CAIRS information retrieval software, therefore, its structure is not so much that of a relational database system as a series of interconnected databases using pointers; data is transferred from one database to another to provide the functionality of an integrated system. Updating is a combination of real-time and batch updating. Functions included in CAIRS LMS are: Cataloguing and enquiry (including OPAC), Circulation, Acquisitions, Serials control and Inter-library loans.

Descriptors — Integrated library housekeeping system; Cataloguing; OPAC; Circulation; Acquisitions; Serials control; Inter-library loans

Operating System — MS DOS; UNIX; OS/2; A variety of other operating systems

Price Range — B/C

Languages — English

Reviews — Ellis, E., Bulletin production using CAIRS. *Library Micromation News*, 34, December 1991.

Perrow, D., Implementing CAIRS-LMS in a small academic library: experience at Templeton College, Oxford. *Program*, 25 (3), July 1991.
Leeves, J., *A guide to inter-library loan management systems*. LINC, 1991.
Marks, C., Inter-library lending packages: a review. *Library Micromation News*, 28, June 1990.
Miskin, C., MicroCAIRS for a legal database service. In Burton, Paul, ed. *MS-DOS software for library and information applications*. Aldershot: Gower, 1990, 39 - 57.
Library management with CAIRS-LMS. *VINE*, 79, 1990.
Smith, N., MicroCAIRS at Simpson Curtis. *The Law Librarian*, 20 (2), 57 - 60.
CAIRS-LMS: a library housekeeping system based on CAIRS. *VINE*, 74, 1989.
Siswell, A., A piece of the automation action. *Library Micromation News*, 20, 1988.

CALM

Supplier — Documedia Systems Ltd

General Details — CALM is a library management system, designed for colleges and special libraries, which supports cataloguing and retrieval, circulation (with a choice of high or low volume loans), acquisitions (full order tracking and cost analysis), serials control and standards management. CALM supports image processing whereby images can be assigned to catalogued items or readers. It is a fully integrated system and is menu-driven. It is a flexible system allowing customisation where required and is well-suited to multi-media applications. Cataloguing is not MARC-based but MARC records can be imported to the cataloguing system. CALM can be single-user or multi-user (using Novell NetWare).

Descriptors — Integrated library housekeeping system; Acquisitions; Cataloguing; Circulation; Serials control; Standards management; Information retrieval; Thesaurus control; Image processing

Operating System — MS DOS

Price Range — C (BASE module)

Languages — English

Reviews — Gillman, P., Cost and effectiveness. *C&L Applications*, 4 (3), October 1990.

CARBON COPY PLUS *

Supplier — Meridian Technology Inc (USA)

European Dealers/Distributors — Relay Communications UK; Microcom UK Ltd

General Details — Carbon Copy Plus is a communications package providing both remote access and conventional communications facilities. Remote access with another computer is achieved if a second copy of the software is present on that computer. Terminal emulation allows communication with online databases, mainframes and bulletin boards.

Descriptors — Communications; Remote access

Operating System — MS DOS

Price Range — A

Languages — English

Reviews — Kittle, P., Remote control software: online from micro to micro. *ONLINE*, 63, September 1989.

CARDBOX-PLUS

Supplier — Business Simulations Ltd

European Dealers/Distributors — IOTA Consultancy (Netherlands)

General Details — Cardbox-Plus is an information management system for microcomputers. It stores records and indexes them for fast retrieval. Databases can contain up to half a million records, each occupying up to a whole screen 36 lines deep and 132 columns wide. Records can be divided into up to 52 fields of any size and shape. In addition, each record can have up to an A4 page of extra free text attached to it. Fields can be variable in length and indexing is flexible: the user controls the terms to be indexed by highlighting them in the record and Cardbox-Plus automatically recognises non-text items such as dates and numbers. Retrieval can be by searching for exact words, approximate words using wild card characters, ranges of words, ranges of numbers and ranges of dates. Boolean operators can be used to combine search terms. Screen display and output formats are user-definable. (See also Picture Cardbox, Cardbox Plus Shell and Term Manager).

Descriptors — Information retrieval; Personal bibliographic database; Reference management

Operating System — MS DOS; OS/2; VMS

Price Range — A/B

Languages — English

Reviews — Hume, S., Software review: Cardbox & ideaList. *ITs News*, 23, Feb 1991, 26-31.
Gillman, P., Building databases. *C&L Applications*, 4 (3), October 1990.
Davies, J., FANGWEL: a program to generate complex author bibliographies from a Cardbox-Plus database. *Program*, 23 (2), April 1989, 189 - 196.
Hume, S., Cardbox Plus: A faithful servant. *ITs News*, 16, May 1988.
Gibson, Clare, Cardbox-Plus: its use in the DOE/DTp Library. *Library Micromation News*, 19, April 1988, 4 - 6.
Cardbox-Plus Information Management System. *Library Micromation News*, 15, January 1987, 3 - 7.

CARDBOX-PLUS SHELL

Supplier — IOTA Consultancy

General Details — Cardbox-Plus Shell is a Graphical User Interface (GUI) for Cardbox-Plus (see Cardbox-Plus). It provides a menu-driven approach for signing onto Cardbox databases with pull-down menus and context-specific Help.

Descriptors — Graphical User Interface; Information retrieval

Operating System — MS DOS

Price Range — A

Languages — English; Dutch

CHIT-CHAT

Supplier — The Sage Group PLC

European Dealers/Distributors — Contact Sage Chit-Chat dealers.

General Details — Chit-Chat is a general purpose communications package designed principally to allow easy connection to and complete file transfer between e-mail, bulletin boards and online systems. A number of terminal emulations are offered, including teletype and viewdata. A range of popular UK modems have been pre-programmed in Chit-Chat: The program is easy-to-use with plenty of help and well-laid-out screens. There is no limit to the number of host profiles which can be set up in Chit-Chat and a phone directory is maintained with host names appearing in alphabetical order. When online, the package is rather limited for interactive online searching, being geared to e-mail and whole file transfer: in particular, the text transfer that online searchers need appears on the menu as "send mail". The "send file" option which many users might expect to use, is not for text uploading. Files cannot be uploaded line by line. The printer is disabled when online. Downloading is activated by the user and data is then captured continuously until the user closes the download file.

Descriptors — Communications; Electronic mail; Online search aid; Viewdata; Downloading

Operating System — MS DOS

Price Range — A

Languages — English

CIBIS (CIPAL BIBLIOTHEEK SYSTEEM)

Supplier — CIPAL

General Details — CIBIS is a local library system with modules for cataloguing, circulation, OPAC, acquisitions and serials control. It is an online and real-time system which can be installed on mini- and micro-computers, using standard Novell software for local networks.

Descriptors — Integrated library housekeeping system; Cataloguing; Circulation; OPAC; Acquisitions; Serials control

Operating System — MS DOS; UNIX; TI-System V; IBM AIX

Price Range — Depends on the configuration and the volume of the library

Languages — Dutch

CLARITY

Supplier — Micronet S.A.

European Dealers/Distributors — Bonntext (Germany); Sismacro (Portugal); Accret (Sweden)

General Details — Clarity is an image storage and retrieval system. It uses state-of-the-art compression techniques for image processing and comes equipped with a powerful word processor, and a data retrieval system with fast response times. Fields and records are variable in length. Features include ability to set up an unlimited number of databases; each database may contain up to 2,000,000 folders; each folder may contain text with variable length up to 16,000 characters and/or graphics up to 255 pages in length; and Boolean retrieval operators.

Descriptors — Image processing; Image retrieval

Operating System — MS DOS

Price Range — C

Languages — Spanish; English; German; Portuguese

CLASS

Supplier — Documedia Systems Ltd

European Dealers/Distributors — DOC 6 (Spain)

General Details — CLASS is a school library management system, derived from CALM (see CALM), which provides multi-media cataloguing and retrieval; acquisitions — with budget controls, orders due and overdue management, and report functions; loans — including overdues and reservations. CLASS supports image processing whereby images can be assigned to catalogued items or readers. CLASS may be single-user or multi-user (using Novell NetWare).

Descriptors — Cataloguing; Acquisitions; Circulation; Image processing; School libraries

Operating System — MS DOS

Price Range — B (single-user); C (multi-user)

Languages — English; Spanish

COLIBRIS *

Supplier — Platinum S.A.

General Details — Document centre management software developed on 4th Dimension, a relational database. Enables each user to set parameters according to his activity. References may be typed manually or downloaded from online database services such as Medline or Biosys.

Descriptors — Information retrieval; Reference management

Operating System — APPLE OPERATING SYSTEM

Languages — French; English

COLOSSUS *

Supplier — Southdata Ltd

European Dealers/Distributors — Imago Logica

General Details — Colossus is an extension to the Superfile database manager, that gives users a text oriented database manager that will handle databases containing several hundred megabytes on PCs with WORM, CD-ROM or magnetic media. It could also allow publishers of large databases to make their products available to the clients at very low cost on WORM disk or CD-ROM. Colossus runs multi-user under MS Net. (See also Superfile).

Descriptors — Information retrieval

Operating System — MS DOS

Price Range — A

Languages — English

Reviews — Heaton, C., Superfile and Colossus in Cambridgeshire libraries. *Library Micromation News*, 27, March 1990.

COMMUNICATOR *

Supplier — Smallsoft

General Details — Launched in 1990, Communicator has been written by information professionals and computer specialists specifically for online searching, and is one of the most comprehensive packages for general online searching needs. In its present version it is most suited to search intermediaries, but there are plans to tailor it more to novice searcher needs in future versions. The program provides menu-driven access and its colour screens make it generally easy to use. Up to 12 host profiles can be set up and stored together with their associated automatic logon routines. A novel feature is the ability for users to set up their own help page for each host profile. Uploading is very flexible — lines are sent one by one and can be viewed at the top of the screen before sending them with a single keystroke. Furthermore, lines can be browsed, sent in any order, repeated or omitted if the strategy needs to be changed. Searches are automatically downloaded into an output file and it is not possible to print while online.

Descriptors — Communications; Online search aid

Operating System — MS DOS

Price Range — A

Languages — English

Reviews — Amitel and Communicator: the new communications packages for online searchers. *Library Micromation News*, 31, March 1991.

CONTACT *

Supplier — X-ON Software Ltd

General Details — This communications package allows access to online, viewdata and E-mail services. Its facilities include VT100 emulation with scrolling windows that will let you capture the text part of incoming data for use with a word processor or spreadsheet. The software also lets you capture information to disk, with the unusual choice of capturing all the information or just the text part of a Viewdata frame or a VT100 connection to a mainframe.

Descriptors — Downloading; Electronic mail; Communications

Operating System — MS DOS

Price Range — A

Languages — English

CONVERT *

Supplier — Southdata Ltd

General Details — Convert takes data from other software such as word processors, databases etc. and converts it for loading into Superfile (see Superfile).

Descriptors — Data reformatting

Operating System — UNIX; MS DOS

Price Range — A

Languages — English

CORA *

Supplier — Harwell Computer Power Ltd

General Details — CORA is a system for the control of files and documents in registries, archives and record management centres. It is based on the STATUS text and information management system. It controls the management of individual documents from their receipt via external or internal mail through to their inclusion into a file and subsequent transfer to other locations. It controls the management of files from their creation in registries and other offices, through to a period in archives and to eventual destruction or transfer. CORA also provides a comprehensive information retrieval system which allows both documents and files to be identified from a wide range of search criteria. The system can be used in its standard format or tailored to meet an individual customer's needs.

Descriptors — Archives; Information retrieval; Records management

Operating System — MS DOS

Languages — English

THE CORPORATE RETRIEVER

European Dealers/Distributors — Intelligent Archive Systems Ltd (UK and Europe)

General Details — The Corporate Retriever is a full text retrieval system written in FORTRAN 77. It runs on a wide range of hardware including mainframes, minis and microcomputers. The program is capable of reading any series II ASCII files. The user can quickly search large amounts of computerised text using single word, a phrase or logical construct. The result of a search will show the number of references, list the file name/document title and then allow you to browse the data and transfer the results or print the screen or entire document. The system uses simple English commands i.e. FIND, LIST, BROWSE, etc. Additional features of The Corporate Retriever are thesaurus, Soundex, truncation, Boolean and proximity searching. The Corporate Retriever has a very low disk overhead (approximately 30% of the data indexed) allowing fast response times. Recent additions to the software include facilities for image retrieval. The Corporate Retriever is one of a number of free text products offered as part of the Cache Document Image Processing product supplied by Intelligent Archive Systems Ltd.

Descriptors — Free Text retrieval; Thesaurus control; Image retrieval; Information retrieval

Operating System — MS DOS; UNIX

Price Range — C

Languages — English

CROSSTALK XVI *

Supplier — Digital Communications Association (US)

European Dealers/Distributors — Softkey (Netherlands); Sold by many dealers in the UK and Europe

General Details — Crosstalk is one of the most well-known communications programs. It is a general purpose package and exists in several different versions: Crosstalk XVI, Crosstalk Mk.4 for more advanced communications, and for each, a networking version. The main supplier in the USA sells worldwide through a distributor network. Although some routines are menu-driven, most of Crosstalk's functions are activated by commands entered next to a prompt at the base of the screen. On-screen help is generally available and colour is used to make the screens easier to use. Host profiles can be stored and automatic logon is available including automatic redial where a logon fails. Uploading facilities are limited to whole file or line by line in sequence. There is more variety in the options for downloading information: this can be continuous, selective, from the buffer or as a single screen dump. Extra features include a good call logging facility which stores information on date, time of day and length of time online, the host service and the number called.

Descriptors — Communications; Online search aid; Downloading

Operating System — MS DOS; MS WINDOWS

Price Range — A

Languages — English

Reviews — Miido, H., Combined use of internal databases, CD-ROMs and online databases: problems and solutions. In *Online Information 89. Proceedings of the 13th International Online Information Meeting. London 12 - 14 December 1989* Oxford: Learned Information, 1989, 349 - 362.
Legott, M., Windows' menu. *Library Software Review*, 9 (1), 1990, 59 - 63.
Lewallen, D. and Dang, L.J., Some DDE functions missing: Crosstalk for Windows 1.0. *PC Week*, 6 (37), September 1989, 66(1).
Simon, B., Crosstalk for Windows offers powerful script language, attractive interface. *PC Magazine*, 8 (17), October 1989, 43(1).

Smith, G., Windows comm market heats up. *PC Week*, 6 (2), January 1989, 25(2).
Jones, R.S., Users choose 'classic' Crosstalk XVI over Mk.4. *InfoWorld*, 11 (1), January 1989.
Plincsar, S.F., Crosstalk and Mirror: what's new under the Crosstalk standard - Part 1. *Online*, 14 (2), March 1990, 46 - 50.
White, F., Crosstalk Mk.4, Version 1.02 (Communications program). *Library Software Review*, 9 (1), 1990, 51 - 54.
White, R., Track CompuServe charges with Crosstalk MK.4. *PC World*, 7 (3), March 1989, 182(3).
Banks, M.A., Crosstalk XVI at your command. (Crosstalk XVI communications software tips). *PC World*, 7 (3), March 1989, 182(3).
Dennis, T., Best comms software. *Which Computer (UK)*, March 1989, 46 - 56.

DARC-CHEMLINK *

Supplier — Telesystèmes Questel

European Dealers/Distributors — Fraser Williams (Scientific Systems) Ltd

General Details — Online search system for searching chemical information on Questel.

Descriptors — Chemical information; Communications

Operating System — MS DOS

Price Range — B

Languages — English; French

DATA MAGICIAN *

European Dealers/Distributors — EPMS bv

General Details — Data Magician is a data reformatting package for microcomputers.

Descriptors — Data reformatting

Operating System — MS DOS

Price Range — A

DATA TREK *

Supplier — Data Trek Inc (US)

European Dealers/Distributors — Data Trek International (France); Data Trek UK; DOC 6 (Spain)

General Details — Data Trek "Manager Series" is a modular library automation system offering cataloguing, circulation, acquisitions and serials control. The modules can be run together or separately. The catalogue features: Boolean searching; five types of printed catalogue; shelf list printing; multiple database creation; subject, author and added entry control; cross references, and catalogue card and label printing. The circulation module controls issue, discharge, reservations and renewals, and generates overdue notices and reports. Barcode capabilities are standard. The ordering of books, journals and reports is controlled by the acquisitions module which features prepayment, invoicing, tracking and receiving orders, fund accounting, electronic transmission or printing of order requests and claim letters, and report generation. The serials module keeps bibliographical and holdings information, supports check-in, claiming, arrival, and renewal alerts, and generates budget reports, overdue reports and printed catalogues. A Databridge module is available for the transfer of bibliographic data in MARC format to the system. Data Trek "Professional Series" is due to be completed in late 1992 and offers handling of MARC records. It also incorporates "Powersearch" which offers text retrieval-type facilities.

Descriptors — Integrated library housekeeping system; Acquisitions; Cataloguing; Circulation; MARC Interface; Serials control

Operating System — MS DOS; APPLE OPERATING SYSTEM

Languages — English; French; Spanish

Reviews — Hoey, P., The Data Trek automated library management system in the Library of the Royal Society of Chemistry. *Program*, 26 (1), January 1992.

DATAFLEX

European Dealers/Distributors — Daustraub Software GmbH (Austria); SYS-DIS (France); Data Access Europe Deutschland GmbH (Germany); LAN Systems SrL (Italy); Eurosoft Norge A/S (Norway); Topis International (Portugal); S.E.I. (Ignacio Megias) (Spain); Eurosoft AB (Sweden); Data Access Europe AB (Sweden); Abacus Research AG (Switzerland); DataFlex Services Ltd (UK)

General Details — DataFlex is a portable applications development tool based on both Relational Database and 4GL technology. DataFlex 3.0 is the first Object Orientated 4GL with a DBMS combining a full-featured object oriented 4GL and User Interface Management System with WYSIWYG application generator. Developers can create complete applications without the need to code. While being a classic 4GL and database, DataFlex is flexible enough to be used as the basis for general information retrieval. Associated products include FlexQL — an SQL-based relational report writer which can be used with a wide variety of DBMS software; XpertRule — a rule based expert systems shell with an Induction Engine allowing both backward and forward chained rules to be derived from examples.

Descriptors — Database management; Information retrieval

Operating System — MS DOS; UNIX (due 1992)

Price Range — Single-user B; Multi-user C

Languages — English; German; Spanish; Italian; Swedish

Reviews — Mill, J., Compliance. *Which Computer*, June 1989

DATATALK

Supplier — Datasoft Ltd

General Details — Datatalk is a general purpose communications package. It offers a range of terminal emulations, including teletype and viewdata and several file transfer protocols for transferring files of confidential data, an optional encryption system is available. The package comes with a number of host profiles already set up, although these are mostly e-mail and bulletin board services. These may be amended, deleted or any number of new profiles may be added. Automatic logon is available together with uploading and downloading. Datatalk has a command language for writing automatic procedures and this also enables a certain degree of customisation of the software.

Descriptors — Communications; Electronic mail; Online search aid; Downloading

Operating System — MS DOS

Price Range — A

Languages — English

DCTS PERIODICALS CONTROL SYSTEM

Supplier — DC Informatik Ltd

European Dealers/Distributors — Norsk Systemutvikling A/S (Norway)

General Details — This is a stand-alone serials control system handling tasks such as check-in, routing of serials, claiming and financial control. It is a flexible system and can be tailored to meet a customer's needs. It is used by customers in Denmark and Norway with collections ranging in size from 175 to 12,000 serial titles.

Descriptors — Serials control

Operating System — MS DOS; UNIX; VAX/VMS

Price Range — C

Languages — Danish; English

DEBORA-DOC *

Supplier — TITE-LIVE S.A.

General Details — No details supplied for this software package.

DIALOGLINK

Supplier — DIALOG Information Services

General Details — DIALOGLINK is a communications package designed for online searching on the Dialog host service, however, it can be used for other hosts as well. Purchasers of Dialog's OnDisc CD-ROM products are also supplied with DIALOGLINK free of charge and it is possible to transfer searches made on the CD-ROM to the online service for more up-to-date searching. DIALOGLINK is provided as two separate elements: the Communications Manager, for online searching, and the Accounts Manager, for recording the costs of searches (this part can only be used with the Dialog service). The Communications Manager comes set up ready for access to Dialog services: users have only to enter their own passwords and telephone numbers to go online. Users in Europe will also have to amend the telecommunications settings. The package can also be used to access up to 20 other online services automatically once a profile has been set up by making selections from various menus and by creating "macros" to store logon procedures. Downloading and uploading facilities are provided by DIALOGLINK and upload files can be transmitted while online and can be edited if necessary. The Accounts Manager can be used to track an online search session on Dialog. This information can be used to generate an invoice that itemises costs and connect times for individual search sessions.

Descriptors — Communications; Online search aid; Downloading

Operating System — MS DOS

Price Range — A

Languages — English

Reviews — Koga, J.S., DIALOGLINK: more shortcuts and quick tips. *Online*, July 1989, 64 - 69.
Koga, J.S., DIALOGLINK: shortcuts and quick tips. *Online*, January 1989, 32 - 39.

DIVA *

Supplier — ANDOR Information Brokers

General Details — A cataloguing and library administration system.

Descriptors — Cataloguing

Operating System — MS DOS

DLIB *

European Dealers/Distributors — D.R.F. van Bremen Informatica Advies bv (Netherlands)

General Details — A Library administration system.

Operating System — MS DOS

DOBILUS *

Supplier — COI-VLABRIC

General Details — No details supplied for this package.

DOCUMENTA *

Supplier — Platinum S.A.

General Details — A document manager which enables each user to set their parameters according to their activity. It is ideal for documentalists but also for anyone who needs to manage information in a professional context.

Descriptors — Reference management; Personal bibliographic database; Information retrieval

Operating System — APPLE OPERATING SYSTEM

Languages — English; French

DV-ONE

Supplier — Chemdata S.A.; Chemdata Iberica S.A.; Chemdata Belgium

General Details — DV-ONE allows the interrogation of a videolink via a microcomputer. The system is made up of a videodisk interfaced with a microcomputer which runs Chemdata's own document management software, TEXTO (see TEXTO). It allows you to mount your own textual, visual and sound databases and search them with an interactive retrieval system.

Descriptors — Information retrieval; Videodisk interface

Operating System — MS DOS; UNIX

DYNIX

European Dealers/Distributors — Dynix Library Systems (UK) Ltd; Dynix Library Systems (Ireland) Ltd; Dynix France

General Details — Dynix is a fully integrated library system, including cataloguing, (MARC and Non-MARC), circulation control, online public access, acquisitions, serials control, community resource and current awareness modules. The system offers variable field lengths, online editing, online help screens and prompts. A comprehensive query language, based on English-like commands is available, together with full management report generation. Full back-up and security is provided. Dynix is used in a variety of library environments including education libraries (eg Universities) and corporate libraries.

Descriptors — Cataloguing; Acquisitions; OPAC; Serials control; Community information

Operating System — PICK

Special Hardware Requirements — Minimum 386 and 486-based PCs.

Price Range — E

Languages — English; Spanish; French; Dutch; German

Reviews — Dynix at the DES. *VINE*, 77, December 1989.

ELROND

Supplier — Head Software International

European Dealers/Distributors — EPMS bv (Netherlands)

General Details — ELROND is a simple but powerful cataloguing/information retrieval system ideal for use in school libraries. It was designed to provide pupils and staff with easy and rapid subject access to the library and resources catalogue by subject keywords, author names, words in titles, Dewey classification etc. ELROND offers five types of search each appropriate to a different level of user skill and complexity of search. The words and terms used in the catalogue can be viewed in a scrolling window and the appropriate one used for a search by pressing one key. The records found can be displayed and printed in various formats ranging from simple author and title lists to the full bibliographic details of a catalogued item. A simple issue system is available for circulation.

Descriptors — Cataloguing; Circulation; School libraries; Information retrieval

Operating System — MS DOS

Price Range — B

Languages — English

Reviews — Pain-Lewins, H. and Watson, L., Microcomputers and school libraries in the United Kingdom: Part 2. *Computers in Libraries*, 10 (2), February 1990.

ENDNOTE

Supplier — Cherwell Scientific Publishing

European Dealers/Distributors — CHEM Research GmbH (Germany)

General Details — EndNote is a personal bibliographic database manager and bibliography maker. It can scan a word-processed document for in-text citations and compile a bibliography from that, using information stored in its database. The EndNote database can contain up to 32,000 characters. It supports a wide variety of bibliographic styles. In addition to the pre-defined styles which automatically come with the software, users can also define their own bibliographic styles. For users who require a more powerful database, EndNote Plus is available which offers more sophisticated searching capabilities. Complementing EndNote is EndLink which translates bibliographic references from online services and other sources of information into a format suitable for use with EndNote. EndLink can be used to import references from online databases into a user's personal EndNote library for use later when citing references in writing.

Descriptors — Personal bibliographic database; Bibliographies; Reference management; Information retrieval; Data reformatting

Operating System — MS DOS; APPLE OPERATING SYSTEM

Price Range — A

Languages — English

EQUILIBRIUM

Supplier — QCL Solutions

General Details — Equilibrium is an integrated library housekeeping system written using the database management system — Informix. The system consists of five main modules covering cataloguing, OPAC, circulation, acquisitions and serials control. The catalogue is the foundation of the system. Data is entered on formatted screens and authority control is provided. Thesaurus creation and control is also available. The record structure is pre-defined though the field names can be library-defined. There are various levels of access to the catalogue for searching ranging from the OPAC to use of the Informix query language for more sophisticated searching. The system is part menu-driven and part command-driven. It is very flexible and capable of customisation.

Descriptors — Integrated library housekeeping system; Acquisitions; Cataloguing; OPAC; Circulation; Serials control; Thesaurus control

Operating System — UNIX

Price Range — C/D/E

Languages — English

Reviews — Callow, M., OPAC at the Home Office using Equilibrium. *VINE*, 84, October 1991.
Callow, M., Equilibrium at the Home Office. *VINE*, 82, April 1991.

ESSENTIAL GUIDE TO DBASE IV IN LIBRARIES - ON DISK *

Supplier — Meckler Ltd

General Details — This two-disk set contains all the program, format, report, label and data files discussed in the book "The Essential Guide to dBASE IV in Libraries". Users may wish to experiment further with the files described in the book. Users may modify and expand upon the programs, making them more suitable for local use. Permission is granted to purchasers of the files on disk to use the program segments that are provided in any way they wish, without restriction. Most users would need to modify them for local practice and probably add features to meet particular needs.

Descriptors — Computer aided learning

Operating System — MS DOS

Price Range — A

Languages — English

EXTRACT *

Supplier — Software Solutions

General Details — EXTRACT is a full text retrieval system providing powerful searching facilities such as use of Boolean logic, proximity searching, word adjacency, index browsing, truncation, internal character masking and range searching. As data is read in, an inverted file is created with unwanted words removed by reference to a stop list. Thesaurus control is also available. Documents retrieved are displayed in their original format with search terms highlighted. The system is menu-driven making it easy to use.

Descriptors — Information retrieval; Free text retrieval; Thesaurus control

Operating System — MS DOS; UNIX

Price Range — C/D

Languages — English

FETCH-IT *

Supplier — Newstar Distribution Ltd

General Details — FETCH-IT is a unique and powerful text retrieval system, developed to provide the most flexible possible approach to analysing textual and/or numeric data. FETCH-IT is capable of processing large amounts of text at impressive speeds. A series of text files can be collected together and indexed as a single library, which can then be subsequently added to, simply by specifying additional file names — there is no need to completely re-index when an addition is made. All words and numbers are indexed as there are no stoplists! Various automated processes are available: batch files, wildcard specification, most recently updated files. Proximity searching and truncation are available. Search output can be directed to a file or a printer. Complex searches on large libraries can automatically gather abstracts (noting source file details) in designated files. Areas of text can be highlighted and sent to the printer, or directly to the keyboard buffer where FETCH-IT is using it's memory resident option. The image options read image files from disk and display the contents at points designated in the text. A hand-held scanner is available to suit the system, supplied with image editing software.

Descriptors — Image retrieval; Information retrieval

Operating System — MS DOS

Price Range — A

Languages — English

FILE REGISTRY SYSTEM *

Supplier — Transaction Point Ltd

General Details — The File Registry System is designed specifically for records managers and file registry workers. Maintains information at file and document level. Manages brought forward and review diaries. Extensive security checking. Supports bar code readers/printers. Multi-user and networking.

Descriptors — Archives; Records management

Operating System — MS DOS

Price Range — C

Languages — English

FILTER

Supplier — Information Automation Ltd

European Dealers/Distributors — EPMS bv

General Details — Filter reformats data to allow the user to copy records in a particular format from one file to a new file in a completely new format. Records can be prepared for reports or an in-house database from sources such as online databases, CD-ROM databases, Database Management Systems and in-house information management systems. A "filter" is constructed incorporating the rules for the conversion process and once this is done the conversion can be run automatically and is easily repeated.

Descriptors — Data reformatting

Operating System — MS DOS

Price Range — A

Languages — English

FINTEK *

Supplier — TH-Data Oy

General Details — No details supplied for this software package.

Operating System — MS DOS

FOLIO VIEWS *

European Dealers/Distributors — Soft Options (Computer Systems) Ltd

General Details — Folio Views combines text retrieval and hypertext technologies with dynamic text editing and offers fast access and flexible management of information. Searching is powerful and facilities to link related information are available. Applications include online documentation, litigation support, electronic and CD ROM publishing, library management, legal and accounting research and customer support.

Descriptors — Database management; Information retrieval; Hypertext

Operating System — MS DOS

Price Range — From price band A depending on number of users

Languages — English

Reviews — Côté, R. and Diehl, S., Searching for common threads. *BYTE*, June 1992. Folio Views 1.3; fast and easy text searching. *PC Resource*, January 1990, 144 - 145.

FREEBASE *

Supplier — CAT Benelux

General Details — FREEBASE is a database management system that is well-suited to literature storage and retrieval. Besides searching with AND, OR and NOT operators, a thesaurus is also available.

Descriptors — Information retrieval

Operating System — MS DOS

Languages — English; Dutch; German; French

FREEFORM

Supplier — Callhaven PLC

General Details — FreeForm is a very fast stand-alone free text retrieval package for PCs and Apple Macs. Retrieval is flexible including searching on keywords, proximity searches and wild cards. The system can also be used in conjunction with MARS (see MARS) to provide free text retrieval alongside its imaging capabilities.

Descriptors — Free text retrieval

Operating System — MS WINDOWS; APPLE OPERATING SYSTEM

Languages — English

FT PROFILE FREEWAY

Supplier — FT Profile

General Details — Freeway is a communications and search interface package developed by FT Profile, the Financial Times' business information service online. Freeway is designed as a stand-alone software package to sit on the user's PC and can be tailored to an individual's own requirements for obtaining information. Using Microsoft Windows 3.0 as its working environment, the package automates logging on, the running of frequently-used searches, the administration of multi-user groups and cost control. It can also guide the user via a series of screens to relevant online sources, assist in constructing searches and help in choosing the most relevant articles to view.

Descriptors — Communications; Online search aid

Operating System — MS WINDOWS

Price Range — A

Languages — English

Reviews — Daniels, M., Search interfaces: the quest of the online virgin. *Electronic Publishing Journal*, Feb/March 1992
Chandler, K., FT Profile Freeway - the road to better online searching ? *Advanced Searcher*, April 1992
Chandler, K., Mark Hepworth - flying the flag for Freeway. *Advanced Searcher*, April 1992.

FULL/TEXT *

Supplier — Fulcrum Technologies Inc

European Dealers/Distributors — C-D Base Ltd

General Details — Full/Text is an information retrieval package which has been available in Europe as an interface to the European legal database, Justis CD-ROM. The system features a graphic interface which was designed specifically to be visually attractive, functional and adaptable. Extensive use is made of colour graphics.

Descriptors — Information retrieval; CD-ROM interface

Operating System — MS DOS; MS WINDOWS; APPLE OPERATING SYSTEM

Languages — English

GEMINI

Supplier — Oy Open Software Solutions AB

General Details — Gemini is an integrated system with modules for cataloguing, acquisitions, circulation and OPAC. Gemini uses the MARC format and data based on the exchange format ISO 2709 with the character set ISO 6937/2 can be transferred into the database. Catalogue entries can also be made manually at the keyboard.

Descriptors — Integrated library housekeeping system; Cataloguing; OPAC; Acquisitions; Circulation

Operating System — MS DOS; MS WINDOWS; OS/2; UNIX

Price Range — C/D

Languages — Swedish; Finnish

GENESYS SIE9751 *

Supplier — Genesys Software-vertriebs GmbH

General Details — The control unit display station Siemens Transdata 9751 consists of two program parts: 1. Genesys SIE9751 allows the communication between a microcomputer and the Siemens mainframe using the x.25 links to packet switching networks, so called Datex-P10, 2. Genesys SIE9751 emulates all functions of a Siemens display station Transdata 9751 on the microcomputer. All keyboard and screen functions of the original display unit 9751 are copied completely. Standard input data can be written by a word processor and stored into a file. All data can be retrieved in a file and/or output on a printer. Characteristic applications for Genesys SIE9751 are online searches with the hosts DIMDI, JURIS and the Umweltbundesamt (INFUCHS), as well as all connections between a microcomputer and a Siemens mainframe.

Descriptors — Online search aid; Communications

Operating System — MS DOS

Price Range — B

GESBIB III *

Supplier — LOGi+

General Details — An information retrieval system with powerful searching capabilities including Boolean query formulation, field directed searching, search refinement, right- and left-hand truncation etc. Up to 100 fields can be defined and all fields can be indexed. Record sizes are limited to 4096 characters per record together with an additional 4096 characters for comments or summary. A wide variety of output formats can be defined for printed reports or production of machine-readable outputs.

Descriptors — Information retrieval

Operating System — MS DOS; OS/2

Price Range — B

Languages — French

GIBUS

Supplier — CeFIS

General Details — GIBUS is a cataloguing and circulation system which has been developed using dBase and is compiled in Clipper. It handles up to 100,000 records and up to 99 copies of each item. The system is available in 3 modules: GIBUS — this is the main module which allows for the cataloguing of books, grey literature, periodicals and articles and manages the thesaurus, circulation, statistics and file maintenance; GIBRE — provides the searching interface (OPAC) and production of bibliographies; GIBAD — for the administration of the database, the modification of parameters and the setting up of passwords. The thesaurus is very flexible: every term can be linked to as many other terms or records as required and synonyms can be added to facilitate access to thesaurus terms and to records. The system is designed to be user-friendly so that non-professionals can use it to run a library or information centre.

Descriptors — Cataloguing; OPAC; Thesaurus control; Circulation; Bibliographies

Operating System — MS DOS

Price Range — A

Languages — French

GOFER *

European Dealers/Distributors — OVM Sopiana Ltd; Riva Ltd

General Details — An information retrieval system which searches all text files without altering them. GOfer can search for text or phrases and these phrases can be connected by AND, OR, NOT or NEARBY (within x number of lines). The text may be blocked, copied to a disk file, or imported to the word processing file in which you may be working. The program reads Word Perfect, Wordstar, Dbase, 1-2-3, Microsoft Word, MacWrite and other files.

Descriptors — File indexing

Operating System — APPLE OPERATING SYSTEM; MS DOS

Price Range — A

Languages — English

Reviews — Miller, M.J. and McCarthy, M., Other text databases: Tornado, Memory Mate, and Gofer. *InfoWorld*, 11 (44), October 1989, 71(2).

GRATEFUL MED

European Dealers/Distributors — The British Library National Bibliographic Service

General Details — Grateful Med is a microcomputer-based software package which provides a user-friendly interface to all the databases on BLAISE-LINK. It was developed by staff at the National Library of Medicine (US). The aim of the program is to simplify searching the BLAISE-LINK databases so that formal training in online techniques is not required. The user is not required to know the formal search language of the BLAISE-LINK system because Grateful Med takes the user through the searching process including formulation of the search strategy, logging on, uploading, downloading and logging off.

Descriptors — Communications; Online search aid

Operating System — MS DOS

Price Range — A

Languages — English

Reviews — Grateful Med now available to Blaise-Link users. *BLAISE SERVICES Newsletter*, 101, Nov/Dec 1989, 6 - 8

GRIPS-LEARN (DIMDI)

Supplier — Information Automation Ltd (IAL)

General Details — GRIPS-Learn provides lessons and searching practice for online searching on DIMDI without online access. It is completely self-contained and requires no previous knowledge of online searching. GRIPS-Learn has instructional, demonstration and practice modes as well as an on screen dictionary. The five lessons introduce DIMDI and DIMDI databases, the GRIPS command language and search strategies. It can be used to train staff, students or library users and will reduce training costs as it is completely self-contained — users have no online use until practised. A junior version (the first three lessons) is also available with an upgrade route to the full version. The junior version includes all standard search commands while the full version includes advanced searching techniques.

Descriptors — Computer aided learning; Training; Communications

Operating System — MS DOS

Price Range — A

Languages — English; German

HEADFAST

Supplier — Head Software International

European Dealers/Distributors — EPMS bv (Netherlands); Winch SrL (Italy); Bibliotheks Centrum Sverige AB (BiC) (Sweden)

General Details — HEADFAST is an information retrieval system designed to be both sophisticated and easy-to-use. It is menu-driven throughout, from setting up a database, to searching and printing out the results. Selections are made using function keys or by selecting from lists by moving an arrow key controlled light bar to the required option. Context specific user-definable help screens can be called from most screens. Up to 100 fields can be defined for each database, each repeatable as required (to a maximum of 255 per database). Records may be as long as required up to a maximum of 32,000 characters. Indexes are created for all the searchable fields and fields can be indexed in a variety of ways. Data entry can be carried out either interactively or offline at the keyboard and batch-updated into the database. It incorporates validation facilities and authority control. Alternatively, data can be uploaded from machine readable sources. There are five main methods of searching ranging from a simple quick search facility to command- and menu-driven searching for more sophisticated users. HEADFAST includes a powerful report generator for formatting retrieved records plus "Virtual Report" facility for immediate links to other software such as desktop publishing. Cut-down versions of HEADFAST are available for use with HEADFAST databases. These provide search-only facilities ideal for use with distributed databases. A CD-ROM interface is available (see HEADFAST/CD) and a loans module is also available for use with HEADFAST.

Descriptors — Information retrieval; OPAC; Cataloguing; Circulation; CD-ROM interface

Operating System — MS DOS

Price Range — B/C

Languages — English; Italian; Other languages user-definable

Reviews — Headfast at Wirral Metropolitan College. *C&L Applications*, June 1992. Headfast: easy to learn. *Information World Review*, May 1989, 22.

Pountain, R., Powerful text retrieval and sophisticated indexing in one package. *BYTE*, August 1990.
Headfast: information retrieval for all. *Library Micromation News*, 25, October 1989.
Baker, J., HEADing for the issue desk. *Library Micromation News*, 26, December 1989.

HEADFAST/CD

Supplier — Head Software International

European Dealers/Distributors — EPMS bv (Netherlands); Winch SrL (Italy); Biblioteks Centrum Sverige AB (BiC) (Sweden)

General Details — HEADFAST/CD is a version of HEADFAST (see HEADFAST) for use with non-updatable CD-ROM data storage. It offers all the search and output features of the standard HEADFAST. HEADFAST/CD provides an easy-to-use searching interface with five searching levels together with flexible outputting capabilities.

Descriptors — Information retrieval; CD-ROM interface

Operating System — MS DOS; MS WINDOWS

Price Range — C/D

Languages — English

HEADFORM

Supplier — Head Software International

European Dealers/Distributors — EPMS bv (Netherlands); Winch SrL (Italy); Biblioteks Centrum Sverige AB (BiC) (Sweden)

General Details — HEADFORM is a generalised data conversion program which reformats data from one format to another. Typical uses include transfer of data from one database system to another; conversion of data downloaded from an online database to be used in a local database system; removal of unwanted data from records downloaded from an online database etc. HEADFORM can ignore unwanted details before, after, between and within data; change the order of fields; allow the user to view and edit the data during the conversion; automatically add data such as constants, dates and incremental numbers; split, combine, repeat or ignore fields in a record.

Descriptors — Data reformatting

Operating System — MS DOS

Price Range — A

Languages — English

Reviews — Sieverts, E.G., Software for conversion of downloaded data; criteria for comparison and assessment. In *Online Information 89; 13th International Online Information Meeting.* Oxford: Learned Information, 1989, 59 - 70.

HEADLINE

Supplier — Head Software International

European Dealers/Distributors — EPMS bv (Netherlands); Winch SrL (Italy); Biblioteks Centrum Sverige AB (BiC) (Sweden)

General Details — HEADLINE was written specifically for online searchers who wanted to access a range of host services. It can be used for any online service that requires teletype terminal emulation. An unlimited number of host profiles can be stored within HEADLINE. These are used in the logging on process which is not automatic. Within the host profile, line parameters are selected from a range of given options and up to 10 stored character strings can be used for various elements of the logon sequence. When logging on, each of the stored strings needs to be triggered as required. Once online, the flexibility of uploading is what would be expected in a package designed for online work. Both the uploading and downloading files can be named and set in operation before going online — this saves costly time when the online connection is open. HEADLINE's default upload method is line by line, each line being triggered as required from the keyboard. It also allows a line to be displayed before transmission and gives the user the option to transmit, skip or hold it for later. Lines cannot be edited while online, but users can type from the keyboard between sending lines from the upload file if they wish, and resend a line if it was transmitted inaccurately. Downloading is continuous, but can be stopped and restarted as often as required during a search — the file is closed automatically when the search is completed.

Descriptors — Online search aid; Communications; Downloading

Operating System — MS DOS

Price Range — A

Languages — English

Reviews — A comparative review of communications packages. *Computers in Libraries (UK)*, 2 (10), June 1989, 7 - 8.
Reid, B.J. and Cameron, A., Headline: software to enhance an online information retrieval service. In *MS-DOS software for library and information applications.* Edited by Paul Burton. Aldershot: Gower, 1990, 24 - 38.

HEADSET

Supplier — Head Software International

European Dealers/Distributors — EPMS bv (Netherlands); Winch SrL (Italy); Biblioteks Centrum Sverige AB (BiC) (Sweden)

General Details — HEADSET combines the editing and variable length capabilities of a word processor with the field-oriented structure required for most text information storage and retrieval systems. Field sizes are user-defined and over 32,000 characters per field are permitted. Other features include: repeating fields; data carry over from one record to the next; automatic generation of dates and sequential numbers; immediate validation of fields and records, and selective or full printing for proof-reading; authority files for vocabulary control. HEADSET may be interfaced with the formats of numerous other software packages and databases using HEADFORM (see HEADFORM). The full data entry facilities of HEADSET are also available within HEADFAST (see HEADFAST).

Descriptors — Data entry

Operating System — MS DOS

Price Range — A

Languages — English

HERITAGE

Supplier — Logical Choice Ltd

European Dealers/Distributors — Business Computers Hilsborough Ltd (N. Ireland)

General Details — Heritage (formerly known as BookshelF PC) is a fully integrated library management system, offering cataloguing, circulation and acquisition modules, to run on affordable PC hardware. The catalogue module deals with every aspect of setting-up a computerised catalogue in the library. Stock is entered by filling in forms on screens which are easy to use or can be downloaded from CD-ROM products like Whitakers Bookbank and BNB (British National Bibliography). Two types of catalogue search are available — an Easy Search for the casual inquirer and the Advanced Search for wider and more sophisticated searching. The circulation module provides fast issue and return of stock by barcode reader or keyboard entry. Reservations and overdues are automatically handled by the software. The acquisitions module is fully integrated with the catalogue. Heritage is installed in a wide variety of smaller libraries in areas such as education, health and commerce.

Descriptors — Integrated library housekeeping system; Acquisitions; Cataloguing; Circulation; School libraries

Operating System — MS DOS; OS/2

Price Range — B/C (depending on the nature of the institution purchasing and the number of users)

Languages — English

Reviews — Pain-Lewins, H. and Watson, L., Microcomputers and school libraries in the United Kingdom: Part 2. *Computers in Libraries*, 10 (2), February 1990.
Pyke, N., In her good books. *Times Educational Supplement*, 12 January 1990.

HYPERKRS *

Supplier — Knowledge Set Corporation

General Details — No details supplied for this software package.

I&D SOFTWARE *

Supplier — Genesys Software-vertriebs GmbH

General Details — Genesys I&D SOFTWARE is a system designed for online information retrieval with microcomputers. The basic version of the software allows micro-to-micro and micro-to-mainframe communication also using asynchronous and x.25 links to packet switched networks. The user can define a variety of communication and terminal parameters such as baud rate, word length, parity and the effect of the break function. Features also included are: functions for the preparation of online input using a standard text editing program; the preparation and storage of search profiles; uploading and downloading, and the post processing of search results. The I&D GRAPHICS SOFTWARE permits the post processing of downloaded search results containing both graphic and textual data. The extended versions of the software include communications links for packet switched networks, mainframe dependent links and the appropriate terminal emulators as for example 3270 terminals. The programs are menu-driven and contain a help function.

Descriptors — Communications; Graphics; Online search aid; Downloading

Operating System — MS DOS; UNIX

Price Range — B/C

IDEALIST

Supplier — Blackwells Scientific Publications

European Dealers/Distributors — MSC Information Retrieval Technologies (Netherlands)

General Details — idealList was developed as an aid to researchers, helping them compile and maintain bibliographies. The format of each record is dependent on the particular application and can be structured or free-form. The user-interface incorporates drop-down menus and supports a mouse. An idealList database can have up to 32,750 records, each up to 65,500 characters long (about 10,000 words). Searching is powerful with optional left and right truncation, wild cards and field-specific searching. Searches can be for words, numbers, dates or number/date ranges and different options on the search menu to find, narrow, widen and exclude represent standard Boolean operators. Cross referencing allows links to be made between records, pointing from a keyword or phrase in one record to another record giving additional information.

Descriptors — Personal bibliographic database; Reference management; Information retrieval; Bibliographies

Operating System — MS DOS; MS WINDOWS

Price Range — A

Languages — English; Dutch

Reviews — Côté, R. and Diehl, S., Searching for common threads. *BYTE*, June 1992.
Pountain, R., Free text retrieval performed the ideal way. *BYTE*, February 1992.
Hanson, T., idealList. *Library Micromation News*, 34, December 1991.

Brown, S., ideaList at BSRIA. *C & L Applications*, 5 (3), October 1991.
Lewis, M., Let the data flow. *PC Magazine*, March 1991.
Hume, S., Software review: Cardbox and ideaList. *ITs News*, Feb 1991, no 23, 26-31.
Holderness, M., Bibliography made cheap. *New Scientist*, 30 June 1990.
Heeks, R., Desperately Seeking Ideas. *The Times Higher Education Supplement*, 15 June 1990.

IMAGE FINDER

Supplier — Imago Logica

General Details — Image Finder is a software program for archiving, retrieving and displaying colour photographs, slides, negatives, video-images and other kinds of images on a PC. Some strong points of the system include: negatives (colour and black-and-white) appear as positives on screen; good picture quality on VGA monitors; professional video quality with extra video monitor; 10-64K storage capacity per image; searching using Boolean operators; searching using list of synonyms; automatic thesaurus compilation; production of instant colour prints of stored images; compatibility with desk-top publishing systems.

Descriptors — Image processing; Image retrieval

Operating System — MS DOS

Price Range — E

Languages — Dutch; English

INFLUX *

Supplier — Dataware

General Details — Influx: recherche documentaire (document retrieval) provides facilities for the storage, modification and retrieval of documents. Influx: bibliothéconomie (library management) covers the function of circulation control and serials control.

Descriptors — Information retrieval; Cataloguing; Circulation; Serials control

Operating System — UNIX

Price Range — D/E

Languages — French

INFOBANK *

Supplier — Information und Kommunikation

General Details — No details supplied for this package.

INFODIAL *

Supplier — Aldoda International Ltd

General Details — Infodial is a communications package designed for online searching. It is built around Crosstalk Mk4 (see Crosstalk XVI) and includes features such as automatic logon; offline preparation of search statements and search routines; flexible uploading; extensive file management facilities for both pre-prepared search strategies and the results of searches; a speedometer indicating the response time of the online service, so that the best times of the day to access it can be chosen.

Descriptors — Communications

Operating System — MS DOS

Price Range — A

Languages — English; French; German

Reviews — Infodial launched. *Information World Review*, December 1989, 37 - 39.

INFODOWN *

Supplier — Information und Kommunikation

European Dealers/Distributors — Wolters Kluwer DSS bv (Netherlands)

General Details — This conversion program can be used in combination with INFOLOG (see INFOLOG) and MIKRO-POLYDOC (see MIKRO-POLYDOC). It can handle input in formats with field tags and convert it to a format with field tags as required for input in a database management program. The user cannot influence the output format, except for the tags themselves. This means that a special version for application with a specific database program must be purchased. Certain fields or specified text strings can automatically be left out, but information from several input fields cannot be merged in a single output field.

Descriptors — Data reformatting

Operating System — MS DOS

Languages — German; English; Dutch

INFOKRAFT LIBRARY SYSTEM *

Supplier — Infokraft Ltd

General Details — Infokraft is a Greek library housekeeping system with modules for storing details of suppliers, cataloguing and enquiry, circulation control and a subject module. The core of the system provides the basic catalogue functions, a subject database and a loans module. Links between modules are fairly limited and fields are fixed length. Data is entered to a formatted screen with full screen editing. There is no provision for subject classification in the cataloguing module — this has to be done in the subject module which will be linked to the cataloguing module in a future release of the software. Searching is in the form of a quick search permitting retrieval by title, book code, author and publisher. A separate searching option offers searching on a range of criteria but there is no provision for the use of Boolean operators. The circulation module provides facilities for issues, returns and renewals and production of overdue reports.

Descriptors — Cataloguing; Circulation

Operating System — MS DOS

Languages — Greek

INFOLINK *

Supplier — Wennergren-Williams Informationssoknung AB

General Details — The software simplifies the routines for database host connection and disconnection by storing logon and logoff procedures, telephone numbers, passwords and search language commands. Up to 30 different search questions can be stored on the software and then uploaded. INFOLINK also includes a function for direct message transfer between terminals. Each software disk has a unique password to protect the access information stored within the program.

Descriptors — Communications; Electronic mail; Online search aid

Operating System — MS DOS

INFOLINK *

Supplier — The Software House

General Details — INFOLINK is a general-purpose communications package for computers running the UNIX operating system. It can access both online hosts and viewdata services and offers facilities for both uploading and downloading.

Descriptors — Communications; Online search aid; Downloading; Viewdata

Operating System — UNIX

Languages — English

INFOLOG *

Supplier — Information und Kommunikation

European Dealers/Distributors — Wolters Kluwer DSS bv (Netherlands)

General Details — INFOLOG is a program that can be integrated with INFODOWN (see INFODOWN) and a database management program like MIKRO-POLYDOC (see MIKRO-POLYDOC). The program is designed for online literature searches and contains features like the ability to store automatic logon procedures and to use function keys to transmit prepared text. INFOLOG is available for text communication, graphics communication and in a networking version. The system is menu-driven and incorporates extensive uploading facilities and flexible downloading facilities. A number of extra features are provided, some within the package and others as optional extras by interfacing to other Info. products. Infolog itself can be set up to allow a number of searchers to use their own password controlled tailored macros for logging on. The system administrator has control over these and can also keep track of which hosts are used by whom.

Descriptors — Communications; Downloading; Online search aid

Operating System — MS DOS

Languages — German; English; Dutch

THE INFORMATION PARTNER

Supplier — New Information Paradigms Ltd

General Details — The Information Partner links packages for desk-top publishing, word processing, text database storage and online communication to automate the process of online searching, downloading and reformatting to produce professional reports. The aim is to quickly and easily produce professional value added reports without having to be a desk-top publishing expert. The system is particularly tailored to business information sources such as Predicasts' PROMT, Infomat, McCarthy, Reuter Textline, ABI Inform, ICC Financial Information, ICC Stockbroker Research, Dun and Bradstreet, InvesText and Kompass.

Descriptors — Communications; Data Reformatting; Downloading

Operating System — MS DOS

Price Range — D

Languages — English

Reviews — Ryan, F., The Information Partner. *Library Technology News*, 3, June/July 1992
Credit Management, May 1992
Aslib Information, 19 (11/12), Nov/Dec 1991
Advanced Searcher, 1 (1), Jan 1991

INFOTRANS *

Supplier — Information und Kommunikation

European Dealers/Distributors — Wolters Kluwer DSS bv (Netherlands)

General Details — No details supplied for this software package.

INMAGIC IMAGE

Supplier — Inmagic Inc (US)

European Dealers/Distributors — Soutron Ltd (UK and Eire)

General Details — INMAGIC Image enables INMAGIC databases (see INMAGIC Plus) to be created incorporating single or multiple images, typically scanned from flat material. Images may be viewed from within the database and manipulated, and are stored in compressed TIFF format. Display can be EGA or VGA. Printing images can be enhanced to 8ppm using video interfacing. Scanning density may be selected from 75 to 300 dpi. The software is of particular value to management of photographic archives, drawings related to patents and trademarks, secure documents, litigation support, and general document management.

Descriptors — Image retrieval; Slide and photo management

Operating System — MS DOS; VMS

Special Hardware Requirements — Appropriate scanner and laser printer together with an adequate storage device (eg WORM)

Price Range — C

Languages — English

INMAGIC PLUS

Supplier — Inmagic Inc. (US)

European Dealers/Distributors — Soutron Ltd. (UK and Eire); EPMS bv (Netherlands); LIS (Netherlands); DOC 6 (Spain)

General Details — INMAGIC Plus is a structured information retrieval system suitable for a wide range of document management applications. Databases are designed by the user by establishing a database structure — the system prompts the user for each field which will make up a database record and instructions are given for the indexing requirements for each field. Fields are variable and unlimited in length and records can be of unlimited size. Searching is both command- and menu-driven and is sophisticated using Boolean logic to combine terms and fields, truncation, phrase and proximity searching, browsing through indexes and pasting terms into searches, and range searching. Searches can be stored and re-used or amended. Search results can be sorted by any of the indexed fields and displayed or printed in a variety of formats defined using the sophisticated report generator.

The number of reports that can be defined is unlimited. Data can be entered at the keyboard using INMAGIC's full on-screen editor (which has authority file and field validation) or imported from machine readable sources if converted to a suitable format (see MARC Adaptor and MULTI Adaptor). INMAGIC FOR LIBRARIES is a pre-defined application of INMAGIC Plus which contains data structures and reports for cataloguing, serials control, routing, bibliographies and circulation. An evaluation version known as TESTMAGIC is available.

Descriptors — Information retrieval; Indexing; Bibliographies; Cataloguing; Serials control; Circulation

Operating System — MS DOS; VMS

Price Range — B/C

Languages — English; Spanish; Dutch

Reviews — Kawamoto, C., Book catalogs using INMAGIC and WordPerfect. *Computers in Libraries*, 10 (11), December 1990.
Velardi, M. and Lafferty, J., MARC and Inmagic: tools for developing an in-house catalog. *Computers in Libraries*, 10 (11), December 1990.
Beiser, K., Inmagic version 7.2. *Computers in Libraries*. 10 (11), December 1990.
Maley, D.B., Inmagic in a small music library. *Library Software Review*, 8 (6), 1989, 350 - 351.
Jones-Randall, K., Developing a microcomputer based index to a local newspaper. *Computers in Libraries*, 9 (6), June 1989, 20-22.

ISIS *

Supplier — B.H. Blackwell Ltd (Periodicals Division)

General Details — ISIS (Integrated Serials Information System) offers ordering, check-in, claiming for missing and damaged issues, in-house circulation, binding control and a variety of management reports. Orders and claims can be electronically transmitted to Blackwells.

Descriptors — Serials control; Online ordering

Operating System — MS DOS

Languages — English

Reviews — Baker, J., ISIS. *VINE*, 78, May 1990

ISYS

European Dealers/Distributors — MSC Information Retrieval Technologies

General Details — Isys is free-text software for MS DOS based PCs.

Descriptors — File indexing; Information retrieval

Operating System — MS DOS

Price Range — A

Languages — English

Reviews — Côté R. and Diehl, S., Searching for common threads. *BYTE*, June 1992.

JISYS

Supplier — K. A. Spencer

General Details — JISys is a Journal Indexing System for all professionals: researchers, lecturers, teachers, doctors, and anyone else concerned with information handling. JISys permits the creation of, and search and retrieval from an individual's own personal journal article database. Facilities include a unique password for data protection and an option to print a fully cross-referenced catalogue of the entire index. JISys is installable on single/dual floppy or hard disk and accommodates up to 10,000 articles (hard disk), up to 10,000 authors per index, a keyword dictionary of 990 words, up to 8 keywords per article, article title up to 158 characters, notes of up to 158 characters and 3 authors per article. (See also VISYS)

Descriptors — Personal bibliographic database; Indexing; Bibliographies; Information retrieval; Reference management

Operating System — MS DOS; RISC OS (Archimedes)

Price Range — A

Languages — English

JLB DOC/JLB BIB *

Supplier — JLB Informatique

General Details — JLB DOC allows the setting up of up to 16 databases defined by the user. Records can have up to 72 variable-length fields with a maximum of 32,000 characters per record. It has an integrated thesaurus including synonym, neighbour, specific and generic relations and can retrieve using character strings. Searching features include use of Boolean logic, right-hand truncation, index browsing etc. 99 output formats are available. All updating is carried out in real time. The system incorporates a videotext interface. JLB BIB provides for general library management and includes the functions of circulation and serials control.

Descriptors — Information retrieval; Cataloguing; Circulation; Serials control; Thesaurus control

Operating System — MS DOS; UNIX

Price Range — D

Languages — French

KAMBIS *

Supplier — Karmac bv

General Details — KAMBIS is a library housekeeping system which provides facilities for cataloguing, acquisitions, serials control, membership registration, circulation control, payroll, accounting, reports and statistics to be integrated in one system. The acquisitions module permits the ordering, receipt, claiming and cancellation of items as well as producing management and financial reports. The cataloguing function is completely based on ISBD rules and allows searching on subject, author, title, serial, genre, ISBN and collection. The circulation control module uses a high-volume transaction barcode scanner which may be used as a stand-alone device, or with a light pen barcode reader. All transactions concerning fines, renewals, acquisitions and reservations are monitored, and the statistics module provides detailed analyses of the usage of the collection.

Descriptors — Integrated library housekeeping system; Acquisitions; Cataloguing; Circulation; Serials control

Operating System — MS DOS

Price Range — D

KAWARE *

Supplier — Knowledge Access International (US)

European Dealers/Distributors — EPMS bv (Netherlands)

General Details — A variety of text and image formats can be managed, distributed and published on magnetic or optical disks using the KAWare system. These formats may be integrated. The product is designed to allow inhouse or commercially valuable information to be accessed in electronic form, without online costs. Customisation and flexibility are key features throughout the desk-top process. Fielded data can be analysed, indexed and then made retrievable in several publisher defined display and print forms. Operation is straight-forward and menu-driven.

Descriptors — Information retrieval

Operating System — MS DOS

Languages — English

KERMIT *

European Dealers/Distributors — King's College

General Details — Kermit is a file transfer protocol which is now implemented on a vast range of mainframe, mini- and micro-computers. Running the appropriate version of Kermit on each of two entirely different types of computer linked by appropriate RS-232 cabling enables files transfers of any file type to be accomplished at speeds of up to 19,200 band. Microcomputer versions all include some form of terminal emulations, however terminal emulation is not its main purpose. The latest Macintosh version is now compatible with the Macintosh II and has a number of additional features including the ability to send all files in a specified folder. Kermit can be used for automatic logging on, uploading and downloading.

Descriptors — Communications

Operating System — MS DOS; APPLE OPERATING SYSTEM

Price Range — Public Domain

Languages — English

KNOSYS

Supplier — Micronet S.A.

European Dealers/Distributors — Bonntext (Germany); Sismacro (Portugal); Accret (Sweden)

General Details — Knosys is a powerful information retrieval system which combines a complete suite of editing functions with a text database program capable of manipulating data contained in variable length fields and records, and accessing information by means of an extensive list of powerful retrieval functions. The system is easy to use with function keys, pop-up windows and point and shoot technology and requires no previous programming experience. Constraints on record size are: maximum record size of 32 Kbytes (approximately 32,000 characters); a maximum of 65,000 records per database;

a maximum of 64 fields per record. A database structure is created by entering the names of the required fields and the manner of indexing for each. Data can be entered into records from the keyboard or imported in a variety of formats. Searching is powerful includes full Boolean logic (AND, OR, NOT), searching across all fields or restricting searches to one or more fields by specifying the field name in the search strategy, range searching, phrase searching and proximity searching, and right hand truncation, either by single characters or a search stem. A synonym facility allows users to define and search groups or words 'similar to' each other. The index can be browsed on the screen while searching and records can be viewed in a list and full format. Further formats can be used to print out records.

Descriptors — Information retrieval

Operating System — MS DOS

Price Range — C

Languages — Spanish; Portuguese; German; English

Reviews — Reviews have appeared in *BYTE*, *Online World Review*, *PC Magazine*, *PC Woche* and *DOS Test*.

KNOWLEDGEBASE *

Supplier — Format Products for Computers Ltd

General Details — Knowledgebase is a powerful software tool for computer-assisted training and open learning. It allows the creation, editing and delivery of words and pictures on any IBM-compatible computer. Knowledgebase might be described as an electronic book: it is the on-screen equivalent of desktop publishing. To create a conventional book, knowledge in the form of words and pictures is transformed and arranged into pages, chapters and volumes. To access the knowledge we can refer to the contents page and index, or browse through the chapters until we find the wanted information. This is how Knowledgebase operates.

Descriptors — Computer aided learning; Image retrieval; Information retrieval

Operating System — MS DOS

Languages — English

LABELMAKER

Supplier — Decision Technology

General Details — Labelmaker is a labelling and barcoding system which supports a wide range of matrix and laser printers. It prints scaleable text up to six inches in height, barcodes, symbols, lines, boxes etc on virtually any stationery. The system includes database facilities.

Descriptors — Labels

Operating System — MS DOS

Price Range — A/B

Languages — English

LANCASTER UNIVERSITY INTER-LIBRARY LOANS MANAGEMENT SYSTEM

Supplier — Lancaster University Library Computing

General Details — An inter-library loan facility offering the following features: Sending of requests; E-mail transmission and receipt; Receipt of incoming items (photocopies, items which can be taken out of the library, items which can be used only in the library); Collection of items i.e. those items which can be taken out of the library; Return of items; Recalls; Renewals; Chasers; Security backup; Archiving of completed requests; Browsing facilities in the requests and archive files, includes browsing via request id (British Library Document Supply Centre number), reader name and bibliographic citation; Management information; User interface to allow writing of routines to collect non standard statistics; Automatic generation of standard letters and reports; Operational manual. The system can be used simultaneously by up to 17 users depending on the hardware and the version of PICK selected. Networks are not required.

Descriptors — Inter-library loans

Operating System — PICK

Special Hardware Requirements — The system runs on IBM PCs and compatibles with the PICK operating system. The appropriate number of extra serial ports must be fitted to the PC to achieve the desired multi-user configuration.

Price Range — C

Languages — English

Reviews — Leeves, J., *A guide to inter-library loan management systems.* LINC, 1991. Marks, C., Inter-library lending packages: a review. *Library Micromation News*, 28, June 1990.

LANSLIDE

Supplier — Lancaster University Library Computing

General Details — Lanslide is a cataloguing and retrieval system for slide libraries. It provides cataloguing with fields for accession number, heading, title, classmark and subject; mini-label production; "keyword" searching (single words or phrases) with Boolean logic and truncation on single words and dates; browsable record display. The "keyword" index is created from all words (except pre-defined stop words) in the heading, title and subject fields. Mini-labels are automatically generated and are suitable for fixing to the mount of a 35mm transparency.

Descriptors — Cataloguing; Slide and photo management

Operating System — PICK

Price Range — B

Languages — English

Reviews — Godfrey, J., A slide library as a teaching resource in art and design education: improving slide retrieval for users. *Audiovisual Librarian*, 15 (4), Nov 1989, 190 - 200.
Clark, W. and Harrison, K., Lanslide: the automation of the University of Lancaster Library's slide collection. *Audiovisual Librarian*, 14 (4), Nov 1988, 196-200.
Harrison, K. and Clark, W., Lanslide: the development of a system for managing a slide collection at the University of Lancaster Library. *Program*, 22 (4), Oct 1988, 365-377.

LEXICON *

Supplier — Dolphin Computer Services Ltd

General Details — LEXICON (formerly ACCESS) is a complete system for the cataloguing, issue, return and renewal of books in a school library. It also has modules for serials control and stock checking. It contains details of all books, all borrowers, books currently on loan and an historical trail of information on book usage. The catalogue can be searched by author, title and subject. An OPAC is available for end-user searching. The normal system assumes a school library with a self-service approach to borrowing, though it can quickly be adapted to suit other environments or methods of use if desired.

Descriptors — Integrated library housekeeping system; Cataloguing; Circulation; OPAC; Serials control; School libraries

Operating System — PICK; UNIX; MS DOS

Languages — English

Reviews — Pain-Lewins, H. and Watson, L., Microcomputers and school libraries in the United Kingdom: Part 2. *Computers in Libraries*, 10 (2), February 1990.
Baker, J., Dolphin Library System. *VINE*, 77, December 1989.

LIB-BASE

Supplier — Lib-BASE

General Details — Lib-BASE is a library housekeeping system providing facilities for book ordering, acquisitions, management of finances, circulation control, cataloguing to full UK MARC standard, printing of barcodes and book spine labels, catalogue searching and printing and serials control.

Descriptors — Cataloguing; Circulation; Acquisitions; Serials control

Operating System — MS DOS

Price Range — C

Languages — English

LIBER *

Supplier — Relais Informatique International

General Details — LIBER is a French library housekeeping system (also marketed in Spain under the name THOT). Functions include serials control incorporating subscription and collection management; acquisitions including budget control; cataloguing compatible with UNIMARC and complying with ISBD standards, retrieval using dedicated screens or Minitel and OPAC — vocabulary control is available during cataloguing; circulation control provides optional use of barcodes; also available are customisable screen and print formats and a variety of other general purpose utilities including stock-taking, inter-library loans and parametrisation. The system is multilingual with a wide variety of language versions available.

Descriptors — Integrated library housekeeping system; Serials control; Acquisitions; Cataloguing; OPAC; Inter-library loans

Operating System — MS DOS; PICK; UNIX

Price Range — D/E

Languages — French

LIBMAN *

Supplier — Amtek Computer Systems Ltd

General Details — LIBMAN is an integrated library housekeeping system suitable for schools and small to medium-sized libraries. The DOS version is written in Clipper; the UNIX version is written in Recital. It incorporates flexible housekeeping options and is easy-to-use with user defined context-specific help.

Descriptors — Cataloguing; Circulation; Community Information; Acquisitions; OPAC

Operating System — MS DOS; UNIX

Price Range — B/C

Languages — English

LIBRARIAN

Supplier — Eurotec Consultants Ltd

General Details — LIBRARIAN is an integrated library administration system currently incorporating: cataloguing; online public access, circulation control, acquisitions, stock control, current awareness and data conversion. Catalogue entries are designed to the requirements of each library, as too are the enquiry access points (eg author, title word, subject, classification, ISBN, year of publication, etc. which may be combined using the Boolean operators AND, OR and NOT). Circulation control information is also user-defined, particularly material/borrower categories and fine/penalty systems. Transactions are barcode driven with a secure audit trail. Public inquirers obtain current loan status/availability of any material which results from an enquiry. Reserved material availability and overdue notices are readily produced. Usage statistics relating to both material and borrowers are automatically maintained by the system. Each module within

LIBRARIAN is menu-driven, requiring only single-key responses. Data entry and amendments are via a simple, form-filling procedure with full editing facilities. Output can be sent to the screen, printer, or disk. Disk output is in a word-processing compatible format. There are no size limitations in the system. Storage capacity is limited only by the amount of hard disk available.

Descriptors — Integrated library housekeeping system; Cataloguing; OPAC; Circulation; Acquisitions

Operating System — MS DOS; Concurrent DOS; Multi-user DR DOS

Price Range — B/C

Languages — English

LIBRARY 2000

Supplier — Elea Ltd

General Details — Library Management System (LMS) is a Greek package which offers a simple library catalogue and loans system. Cataloguing is basic, providing the necessary bibliographic information for the loans function. Searching is possible by author, ISBN, publisher, title, subject and code number. A suppliers file is maintained and can be used in conjunction with acquisitions. Relative information about outstanding invoices, purchasing costs can be retrieved. Further enhancements to this function are planned for the Autumn 1992. An inter-library loans module is due to be released in 1993. LIBRARY 2000 is compatible with BIBLIOGRAPHY 2000 which is the first Greek Books in Print electronic database and records can be downloaded directly into the library system.

Descriptors — Cataloguing; Circulation; Acquisitions

Operating System — MS DOS; UNIX

Price Range — B

Languages — Greek

LIBRARYPAC 1

Supplier — Information Systems Design

General Details — LibraryPac 1 is a software package used for the storage and retrieval of bibliographic or text-based information. It offers the flexibility common to text retrieval software, providing the end-user with the tools for defining and accessing the database. Users can set up their own record structure to suit their own particular needs. The maximum record size is two screens (36 lines) on which up to 127 fields can be defined. Fields are variable in length, empty fields are not stored and indexing instructions for each field are defined by the user. Data entry is online with full screen editing. There is no form of authority control or thesaurus facility. For printed output, a report generator is available to enable the user to define the format in which records should be printed. Searching is command-driven and allows for the use of Boolean operators, nested Boolean logic, truncation and field-specific searching. The system permits the index to be viewed and browsed. Versions of LibraryPac are also available which add circulation control to the cataloguing and retrieval functions (See LibraryPac 2 and LibraryPac 3).

Descriptors — Cataloguing; Information retrieval

Operating System — MS DOS

Price Range — A

Languages — English

LIBRARYPAC 2/LIBRARYPAC 3

Supplier — Information Systems Design

General Details — LibraryPac 2 provides all the functions of LibraryPac 1 (see LibraryPac 1) for the storage and retrieval of catalogue records, but in addition adds a circulation control module. This offers facilities for issue, return, renewal and simple reservations together with production of letters and some statistics. The system is command-driven with input either from keyboard or barcodes (barcode printing and barcode transaction processing is provided). Parameters for loan periods and borrower privileges are established on a matrix basis during configuration and timings for the production of overdue letters, reservations etc are user-defined. Integration with the cataloguing module is relatively limited since the circulation status/availability of an item cannot be viewed from the catalogue. LibraryPac 3 provides all the functions of LibraryPac 2. In addition, up to four barcode data capture units can be connected via Piconet Serial modules for processing circulation transactions and a network version is available. LibraryPac 2 can be upgraded to LibraryPac 3 for the difference in price.

Descriptors — Cataloguing; Circulation; Information retrieval

Operating System — MS DOS

Price Range — B

Languages — English

LIBRI *

Supplier — D.I.C.E. Ltd

General Details — LIBRI is a cataloguing, enquiry (OPAC) and circulation system. It is written in Clipper with many additional routines written in Assembly and C. Its screens include helpful prompts to the user but no other on-screen help is available. The catalogue structure is fixed and records are held at the title level with linked copy information. Authority files can be maintained for certain fields: personal names, corporate names, publishers, serial titles, series titles and subjects. Most fields are searchable and during searching, authority lists can be displayed and terms selected for use within search statements. Only the Boolean operator 'AND' can be used to combine search terms. The circulation function provides facilities for issues, returns and renewals and produces reports listing overdue items. It does not provide circulation statistics or reservations. LIBRI runs with Greek language screens but can handle data in both Greek and Latin characters. Screens can be provided in other languages on request to the supplier.

Descriptors — Cataloguing; Circulation

Operating System — MS DOS

Languages — Greek

LIBRIS

Supplier — Mercury Design (Burningbow Division)

General Details — Libris is a system designed for schools and is aimed at introducing students to the use of computers in the library together with barcode technology. (The Barcode wand, de-coder PC card and Barcode printing software is inclusive in the package.) Libris is a complete library housekeeping system including circulation, cataloguing, reservations, renewals and overdues. There are fully customised facilities for the printing of both overdue and reservation notices. Searching is possible by author, title, keyword, subject, truncated title etc. Extra search facilities may also be networked enabling students to search materials without affecting the system or interrupting the librarian. Separate add-on modules are available to handle charts, maps, videos, tapes etc.

Descriptors — School libraries; Integrated library housekeeping system; Cataloguing; Circulation

Operating System — MS DOS

Price Range — B

Languages — English

Reviews — Hines, E., Light Reading. *Times Educational Supplement*, March 20, 1992. Mabey, M., Impressions of LIBRIS. *Library Micromation News*, 34, December 1991.

LICON

Supplier — Floyd Ratcliffe Consultancy Services Ltd

General Details — LICON is a menu-driven library housekeeping system available as a standard package, or as a customised version. Functions include cataloguing and enquiry, circulation control, acquisitions, serials control and accounting. A standard set of fixed-length bibliographic fields are available for cataloguing and data is entered to a formatted screen with full screen editing (data is entered in upper case). The catalogue module is indexed on accession number, Dewey number, ISBN, title, series, two author fields, publisher, and six subject fields where some subject control is available. Searching incorporates the use of Boolean operators to combine search terms and fields and records can be displayed and browsed through in a number of different formats. The circulation module allows for the issue, return, renewal and reservation of items; overdues can be chased and limited parametrisation is possible allowing the library to set a standard loan period and a standard number of items which can be borrowed by a single user. The acquisitions module allows for creating new orders, receiving items on order, maintaining a suppliers file and chasing outstanding orders. Serials control is an optional additional module.

Descriptors — Integrated library housekeeping system; Cataloguing; Circulation; Acquisitions; Serials control; School libraries

Operating System — MS DOS

Price Range — LICON Junior - A; LICON multi-user - C; LICON customised - E

Languages — English

LITREF *

Supplier — April Computing Executive Ltd

General Details — LITREF is a micro-based literature reference database written in dBase and Clipper. It is capable of importing data from mainframe computers using a file conversion routine provided as part of the package. Information may also be input through the keyboard using a data input form consisting of 10 fields which has to be used for all types of document reference. It is possible to store information in any number of databases. These databases can be merged, search results routed to a different or new database, deleted, output to screen or printer, or exported to text files. Search facilities include: indexed searches on author or keyword fields; sequential searching on any field except the abstract, and the narrowing down of searches by performing a new search on the set of records retrieved. This procedure may be repeated an unlimited number of times. A basic report generator permits the production of reports and bibliographies.

Descriptors — Personal bibliographic database; Information retrieval; Reference Management; Data reformatting

Operating System — MS DOS

Price Range — A

Languages — English

Reviews — Hanson, T., LITREF. *Library Micromation News*, 29, Sept 1990.

LIVELINK *

Supplier — Photobase Ltd

European Dealers/Distributors — Audio-Visual Organisation

General Details — Livelink allows for the storage and retrieval of photographic and other images within Superbase 4, the fully relational Windows database. Flexibility and ease of use are achieved by capturing images from a variety of video sources. Video capture is instantaneous and images are dynamically compressed and decompressed in real time from within the application.

Descriptors — Image processing; Image retrieval

Operating System — MS WINDOWS

Special Hardware Requirements — Colour VGA display for 640 * 480 mode; 2 Mb RAM; Mouse.

Price Range — B (Software only)

Languages — English

LOGABIB *

Supplier — Info 3 D

General Details — A real-time library housekeeping system with modules offering cataloguing (multi-media) and retrieval, circulation and Minitel. The system is compatible with UNIMARC.

Descriptors — Cataloguing; Circulation

Operating System — MS DOS; UNIX

Price Range — E

Languages — French

LOGOTEX

Supplier — Chemdata S.A.; Chemdata Iberica S.A.; Chemdata Belgium

General Details — LOGOTEX is a programming language which does not require any particular programming experience. It allows the generation of menu-driven applications by front-ending TEXTO commands (see TEXTO). Examples of applications: Menu-driven searching (allowing access to TEXTO databases by users who are not familiar with either the software or with the files); Videotext searching; Menu-driven input and data validation; Thesaurus; Interfacing to peripheral devices. LOGOTEX is available on more than 20 different operating systems. LOGOTEX is sold exclusively to TEXTO users.

Descriptors — Database management; Information retrieval

Operating System — MS DOS; UNIX

Price Range — C

Languages — French; English; German; Spanish; Italian; Portuguese; Russian; Arabic

MABB

Supplier — Meester Automatisering

General Details — MABB (Meester Automatisering Bibliotheek Beheer) is a cataloguing and circulation system which offers very fast searching using indexed search files. Screens are ergonomic with the use of reference windows where relevant, context-sensitive help screens and minimum training required. A variety of media types can be stored in the catalogue and searching can use title words, author names, keywords, publisher, city of publication, organisation etc. Facilities for circulation, subscriber administration, import of external files and networking are also available.

Descriptors — Information retrieval; Cataloguing; Circulation

Operating System — MS DOS

Price Range — B

Languages — Dutch

MAC SCHOOL LIBRARY

European Dealers/Distributors — Celtip Computers (UK and Europe)

General Details — Mac School Library is part of an integrated schools administration package but it has been designed to run as a stand-alone product. It has been produced solely for the Apple Macintosh. It runs either single- or multi-user with AppleShare. Upgrading at a later date is a simple process. CSL Library allows a school to track up to 65,000 books and up to 5,000 borrowers. Records can be keyed in, transferred from an ASCII file or downloaded from MARC format. There is a wide range of finding and searching procedures with special simplified ones for students. Circulation control facilities include tracking overdues and monitoring borrower privileges. It also has facilities for using a light pen for checking books in and out. The system prints book labels and catalogue cards. It has comprehensive reporting options which include printing bar codes. The program maintains a wide range of statistical information on circulation and borrowers. Mac School Advance Booking runs on similar lines to the Library Module but it has the facility to pre-book items and so is particularly useful for audio visual aids, tapes, films etc.

Descriptors — School libraries; Cataloguing; Circulation

Operating System — APPLE OPERATING SYSTEM

Price Range — A/B

Languages — English; French

MACREX INDEXING PROGRAM

Supplier — Macrex Indexing Services

General Details — Macrex is a program designed to assist an indexer working from a manuscript, printed proofs or an already completed book. It allows for entry, verification and comprehensive editing of index items, which are instantly visible on screen in sorted order in an indented format. Data is sorted according to any chosen convention (the default is British Standard). Final copy can be printed or sent to a disk file in almost any layout defined by the user or chosen from style sheets provided. Run-on and set-out subheadings and any combination of the two are accommodated. Files can be automatically transferred to a wide range of word-processors and desk-top publishing systems. A wide range of accented characters are supported and characters outside normal code-pages can be drawn and defined by the user. Input can be from ASCII files as well as the keyboard and provision is made for conversion of existing indexes on disk (including those generated by the automatic indexing modules attached to word-processing programs) to Macrex format for further manipulation including editing, accurate sorting, merging and printing. Automatic cumulation of any number of index files; entries from a section or chapter can be extracted to make separate indexes. Capacity is in excess of 500,000 lines, depending on hardware used. Macrex is used to prepare the indexes for some of the world's leading journals and the manuals of major software companies. It was also used to index the 1988 revision of BS3700 (the British standard on indexing).

Descriptors — Bibliographies; Indexing

Operating System — MS DOS; OS/2

Price Range — A

Languages — English

Reviews — Fetters L.K., Macrex 4. *American Society of Indexers Newsletter* March/April 1989

MACTERMINAL 2.3 *

European Dealers/Distributors — Apple Computer UK Ltd

General Details — MacTerminal is a multi-function terminal emulator that allows a Macintosh to emulate a Digital VT100 or TTY terminal. It also provides file transfer support for XModem and MacBinary file formats. It provides a high level of support for Apple's own Hayes-compatible modem, but can also operate with other UK modems.

Descriptors — Communications

Operating System — APPLE OPERATING SYSTEM

Price Range — A

Languages — English

MAGICKEY *

Supplier — EPMS bv

General Details — MagicKey is a small program which can be used in conjunction with Inmagic (see INMAGIC PLUS) to enhance its editing facilities. It also incorporates a number of features which speed up entry and exit of Inmagic together with movement between its various environments using a hotkey facility.

Descriptors — Data entry

Operating System — MS DOS

Languages — Dutch; English

MARC ADAPTOR

Supplier — Inmagic Inc. (US)

European Dealers/Distributors — Soutron Ltd (UK and Eire); EPMS bv (Netherlands)

General Details — MARC Adaptor converts bibliographic records in USMARC format into INMAGIC format, ready to be loaded into an INMAGIC database (see INMAGIC Plus). The MARC Adaptor makes it easy to acquire cataloguing information from a variety of sources and to build an online catalogue with a minimum of effort together with INMAGIC. MARC Adaptor can be used with USMARC/OCLC MARC formats for several types of materials including books, serials, visual materials/audio-visual media, archives, manuscripts, music/scores and sound recordings. With the MARC Adaptor it is possible to choose what MARC information is extracted and converted. A Field Map is defined and this specifies how information will be arranged in each INMAGIC record.

Descriptors — MARC-Interface; Data reformatting

Operating System — MS DOS

Price Range — A

Languages — English

MARS

European Dealers/Distributors — Callhaven PLC (UK)

General Details — MARS (Multi-user Archival and Retrieval System) is an easy to use but powerful document imaging system. It provides exceptionally fast and flexible retrieval of documents, whether from paper, microfiche, microfilm, sound or video - as well as retrieval of computer files from any computer system. It is an open, flexible means of accessing any information from any source. MARS has been used by many Fortune 50 companies for document imaging, usually in high-volume, heavy-usage, multiple-site environments, and it has proved itself to be reliable and resilient in real-world situations. One of the reasons for its ease of use is the MARS interface which can be reconfigured for every user. MARS is also equipped with a robust applications programming interface (API) called Shuttle, which enables MARS to be linked to many other programs.

Descriptors — Image processing; Image retrieval

Operating System — APPLE OPERATING SYSTEM; MS WINDOWS

Special Hardware Requirements — Minimum configuration Mac LC or PC 386 with 6Mb RAM

Price Range — E

Languages — English

MASS BREAKOUT *

Supplier — PC Communications Ltd

General Details — Offers all the features of Breakout, with additional facilities for multi-tasking and in-built word processing. Mass Breakout's powerful programming language, IQ, enables the user to totally automate and customise communication tasks. For example the software can be programmed to automatically download selected information from an online host at specified time intervals. An internal or external modem is supplied as part of the Mass Breakout package.

Descriptors — Communications; Online search aid; Viewdata; Downloading

Operating System — MS DOS

Price Range — B/C

Languages — English

MASTERFILE II/III

Supplier — RISC Developments Ltd

General Details — This is a general purpose database allowing large amounts of information to be stored, amended, sorted and printed etc. MASTERFILE is easy to use and is suitable for use in home, office or school.

Descriptors — Database management; School Libraries

Operating System — RISC OS

Special Hardware Requirements — Hardware must be Archimedes, A3000 and A5000 machines running RISC OS 2 or later and RAM must be at least 1 Mbyte.

Price Range — A

Languages — English

MDUP

Supplier — Barcelona Tecnologia, S.A.

General Details — MDUP was originally developed by the Universitat Politecnica de Catalunya, Spain, as a complementary system to a large VAX-based system which the university was also working on. The system has facilities for MARC cataloguing.

Descriptors — Cataloguing

Operating System — MS DOS

Languages — Spanish

MEDIA-BOP *

Supplier — ISL

General Details — Media-Bop is an integrated software package which can be acquired in modules which include circulation, cataloguing and retrieval and acquisitions. Cataloguing is compatible with UNIMARC and authority control is available on author and material fields. The system is designed to suit multi-media applications and searching (title, author, keywords fields) can be on all media types or limited to a specific type.

Descriptors — Integrated library housekeeping system; Cataloguing; Acquisitions; Circulation

Operating System — UNIX

Languages — French

MEMOLOG 2 *

Supplier — CRDP

General Details — An information retrieval system which is provided with a thesaurus from CNDP:MOTBIS.

Descriptors — Information retrieval

Operating System — MS DOS

Price Range — A

Languages — French

MEMORY MATE

Supplier — Shareware Marketing

General Details — Memory Mate is a free form text retrieval system with forms, dates and hypertext capabilities. It is memory resident, requiring 90K of free memory. It supports multiple databases and wild card searches. It is well-suited to keeping notes, memos, tables, statistics, lists etc.

Descriptors — Information retrieval; Hypertext

Operating System — MS DOS

Price Range — A

Languages — English

Reviews — Miller, M.J. and McCarthy, M., Other text databases: Tornado, Memory Mate, and Gofer. *InfoWorld*, 11 (44), October 1989, 71(2).

MICRO CDS/ISIS

Supplier — UNESCO

European Dealers/Distributors — Université Catholique de Louvain (Belgium); Royal School of Librarianship (Denmark); German Commission for UNESCO (Germany); D.B.A. Associazione per la documentazione le biblioteche e gli archivi (Italian User Group); UNESCO Centrum Nederland (Netherlands); Biblioteca Nacional, Divisao de Informatica (Portugal); Instituto de Informacion y Documentacion en Ciencia y Tecnologia (Spain); D.A.F.A. Data AB (Sweden); Institute of Development Studies (UK)

General Details — Micro CDS/ISIS is a microcomputer-based information storage and retrieval system produced by UNESCO. It is available at distribution cost only for non-commercial purposes. It has modules for database structural definition, database backup, data entry and modification, and for search, sort, display and print. The system is menu-driven. The user may define a stop word list, and design input worksheets and as many display/print formats as are required. Specifications can be given in the fields to ignore or substitute certain words, numbers or articles for filing of entries without any visible trace of it in the final output. Menus, system worksheets and messages are multi-lingual. Searches are formulated using Boolean logic, proximity operators, field qualification and right hand truncation. Micro CDS/ISIS is the microcomputer equivalent of the CDS/ISIS package which runs on IBM mainframes. There are over 7,000 copies of the micro version in use worldwide.

Descriptors — Information retrieval; Reference management; Personal bibliographic database

Operating System — MS DOS

Price Range — A - covers costs only.

Languages — English; French; Spanish

Reviews — Buxton, A.B., Mini-Micro CDS/ISIS. *Library Micromation News*, 34, December 1991.
Nieuwenhuysen, P., Computerised storage and retrieval of structured text information: CDS/ISIS version 2.3. *Program*, 25 (1), 1991.
Chaudhry, A.A., Adapting CDS/ISIS to index hyphenated and numeric words and incorporating case sensitive storage and retrieval. *Program*, 24 (4), 1990.
Goyal, R.K. and Kumar, S., dBase to CDS/ISIS: a program to convert data from dBase/foxBase to CDS/ISIS. *Program*, 24 (2), April 1990, 181 - 186.
Hopkinson, A., CDS/ISIS information. Regular column in: *Information Development*.
Janssens, D. and Jesse, A., *Micro-ISIS training course*. Geneva : International Labour Office, 1989.
Miido, H., Combined use of internal databases, CD-ROMs and online databases: problems and solutions. In *Online Information 89. Proceedings of the 13th International Online Information Meeting. London 12 - 14 December 1989*. Oxford: Learned Information, 1989, 349 - 362.
Shailendra, K., Neogi, R.N. and Gogia, K.L., Use of CDS/ISIS for creating India's database of serials. *Program*, 23 (3), July 1989, 287 - 294.

MICRO-LIBRARY-SYSTEM (MLS)

Supplier — Top-Tech-Systems

General Details — MLS is a fully comprehensive library management system, written in Clipper and designed specifically for small to medium-sized libraries. It includes all the necessary routines to completely automate cataloguing and enquiry, circulation, acquisitions and library statistics. The cataloguing module is well-designed for multi-media requirements even including a colour option so that screen displays have different colours according to media type. Retrieval includes keyword and Boolean searching. The circulation module is comprehensive, controlled by library-defined parameters and incorporating a short-term-loans facility and statistics. Other facilities include a wordprocessor and the "system-monitor" which monitors how the library is being used on a monthly basis throughout the year. This enables the librarian to allocate the library budget in the most effective way. Graphical analyses are included. MLS can be adapted to any type of library — schools, colleges, hospitals, departmental, etc.

Descriptors — Integrated library housekeeping system; Cataloguing; Circulation; Acquisitions; School libraries

Operating System — MS DOS

Price Range — B (for all modules)

Languages — English

MICRO-OCP

Supplier — Oxford University Press

General Details — Micro-OCP produces word lists, and concordances from texts in a variety of languages and alphabets. It is a versatile tool for anyone involved in the close study of text. Micro-OCP is a further development of its parent mainframe package, the Oxford Concordance Program (OCP) but it has been adapted and made easier to use for those with little or no experience of computing or text analysis. Micro-OCP offers the following facilities; Word lists (lists of words together with their frequencies); Indexes (lists of words together with their references and their frequencies); Concordances (lists of words together with the context that surrounds them, their references and frequencies); Vocabulary Statistics (frequency profile giving cumulative totals relative frequencies type/token ratio).

Descriptors — Indexing

Operating System — MS DOS

Price Range — A

Languages — English

MICRO-OPC *

Supplier — Pica

General Details — Pica is a cooperative non-profit organisation for libraries and other information providing institutions based in the Netherlands. In addition to offering systems on the central Pica computer, Pica has also developed a Local Library System which runs on Micro Vax computers and a Micro OPAC for users with PCs who only want to automate the cataloguing process. It can be used in combination with the Online Shared Cataloguing System to make the local (special) catalogue machine readable.

Descriptors — OPAC; Cataloguing

Operating System — MS DOS

Languages — Dutch

Reviews — Feijen, M., Pica library systems: the third generation. *Program*, 25 (2), April 1991.

MICRO-QUESTEL *

Supplier — Telesystèmes Questel

General Details — Micro-Questel offers online access to the QUESTEL host system and bilingual management of databases using a microcomputer, from acquisition of documents up to search and screen display and print-out. One database can be maintained with up to 100 subfiles, 300 fields, 1,314 characters per field, 10,000 characters per record and up to 200,000 records. To enable sophisticated searching and editing, the documents are composed of a list of several independent headings, the characteristics of which (length, type of contents, etc.) may be modified by the user. Search features include use of Boolean logic, nesting, word adjacency, right-hand truncation, index browsing, range searching etc. Records can be displayed and printed using user-defined formats and indexes including postings can be printed or displayed. Access to the information in the database may be restricted by a password.

Descriptors — Communications; Downloading; Online search aid; Information retrieval

Operating System — MS DOS

Price Range — C

Languages — French; English

MICRO-VTLS

Supplier — VTLS Inc (US)

European Dealers/Distributors — VTLS Inc (Spain); ADDA, SCP (Informàtica Sarrià) (Spain); VTLS of Finland Oy; SWS SoftWare Systems AG (Switzerland/S. Germany)

General Details — Micro-VTLS is a smaller version of VTLS (the large library housekeeping system) and integrates cataloguing, public access catalogue, circulation and statistical reporting functions to support basic library operations. It links VTLS libraries via a modem or direct connect cable to allow online downloading of MARC records. Interfaces to LC, BiblioFile, OCLC, RLIN, WLN, UTLAS and MiniMarc are optionally available and records may also be entered at the keyboard. The circulation module supports full loans facilities including issues, returns, reservations, renewals and fines. The OPAC provides end-users with easy access to the catalogue via fields such as author, subject, title, series, ISBN, and keywords (using Boolean operators). Circulation and catalogue modules can be purchased separately. Menu driven programs are included to perform tasks such as disk formatting and routine data back up. Full image and sound recording is supported by Micro-VTLS. Comprehensive online help screens and online documentation are also available.

Descriptors — Integrated library housekeeping system; Cataloguing; OPAC; Circulation

Operating System — MS DOS

Price Range — D

Languages — 16 languages with easy translation to any European language and multiple character set support

MICROBES *

European Dealers/Distributors — Royal School of Librarianship (Denmark)

General Details — No details supplied for this software package.

MICROFIND *

Supplier — Z A G Computing

General Details — No details supplied for this software package.

MICROLINX

Supplier — Faxon Europe bv

European Dealers/Distributors — Faxon UK Ltd

General Details — MicroLinx is a self-contained serials management system designed for IBM-PCs and compatible computers and developed by the serials subscription agent — Faxon. It provides for check-in and record maintenance, automatic claiming, the printing of binding slips, routing and printing route slips, management and statistical reports sorted in many different ways, comprehensive holdings lists and summary holdings for public service use. Separate modules offer routing list management and union list functions. A library's serials records may be entered manually or downloaded from Faxon's databases for subscriptions which are ordered via Faxon.

Descriptors — Serials control

Operating System — MS DOS

Price Range — C

Languages — English

Reviews — Shields, M. and Woodward, H., MicroLinx: the Faxon Serials Management System. *VINE*, 87, June 1992.
Norman, J., MicroLinx at Loughborough University of Technology. *Library Micromation News*, 24, June 1989.

MICROMASTER *

Supplier — Kommunedata

General Details — No details supplied for this software package.

MICROPHONE II *

Supplier — Computers Unlimited

General Details — MicroPhone II is an advanced telecommunications package providing emulation for VT52 and VT102 terminals and including full-featured scripting facilities. A reduced-function version known as MicroPhone I is also available.

Descriptors — Communications

Operating System — APPLE OPERATING SYSTEM

Price Range — A

Languages — English

Reviews — Bjorner, S.N., In search of the ideal Macintosh software. *ONLINE*, 51, May 1991.

MICROSOFT-ACCESS *

European Dealers/Distributors — Softkey (Netherlands)

General Details — Microsoft-ACCESS is a communications program providing standard communications features. Automatic logon procedures can be stored and user defined menus may facilitate online sessions if a variety of different host computers is accessed.

Descriptors — Communications

Operating System — MS DOS

Languages — English

MIKRO POLYDOC *

Supplier — AB Foretagssimulering; Norsk Senter for Informatikks A/S

European Dealers/Distributors — Wolters Kluwer DSS bv (Netherlands); NIC Nordic Info Center A/S (Denmark)

General Details — Information storage and retrieval system which allows a maximum of 5 databases per system, and a maximum of 32,768 records or 8,300,000 characters per file. There are no limits to the number of characters per record. Each record may be divided into 20 different fields. The user can define field names and abbreviations, and define which fields in the database are to be field, subfield, full text or free text searchable. A generator may be used to produce indexes from the entire database or from parts of it. KWAC indexes are produced from fields or subfields, and KWOC indexes of words in a text. The layout of the indexes is designed by the user. Searching facilities include use of Boolean logic, word adjacency, right-hand truncation, range searching etc.

Descriptors — Information retrieval

Operating System — MS DOS

Price Range — C

MIKROMARC *

Supplier — Norsk Systemutvikling A/S

European Dealers/Distributors — Langlet Informatik (Denmark); Bibliotheks Centrum Sverige (BiC) AB (Sweden)

General Details — MikroMARC is a well-established cataloguing and retrieval system which is MARC compatible. A circulation system and OPAC is also available with the system. Data entry is on simple screens with layouts similar to a catalogue and context-specific help. The search language is based on CCL (a command language close to normal English) with help screens to guide the user. Records can be output in a variety of formats and import/export facilities are available. There are MikroMARC customers in Norway, Denmark, Hungary, Iceland, Sweden, UK and Germany.

Descriptors — Information retrieval; Cataloguing; OPAC; Circulation; MARC-Interface

Operating System — MS DOS

Languages — Danish; English; German; Hungarian; Icelandic; Norwegian; Swedish

MIKROTEL

Supplier — ESRIN (Italy)

European Dealers/Distributors — Cobidoc bv (Netherlands); ESA-IRS national centres or agents; IRS-Dialtech (UK)

General Details — Developed by ESA-IRS, Mikrotel is a communications software package which provides links to the various online hosts. Automatic procedures can be set up which log the user into the chosen host at the touch of a button; programme function keys are available linked to user-definable commands; uploading and downloading can be done with ease. It is possible to enter DOS whilst still in Mikrotel and from there the colours displayed on the screen can be changed. Mikrotel allows VT-100 emulation, the use of COM1 and COM2 ports and the use of XMODEM and KERMIT protocols. An online help facility and a comprehensive manual complete the software.

Descriptors — Communications; Online search aid; Downloading

Operating System — MS DOS

Special Hardware Requirements — Asynchronous communications adaptor, 256K RAM

Price Range — A

Languages — English

MILL-IV *

Supplier — Portsmouth Polytechnic

General Details — MILL is an inter-library loans management package written in dBase IV. It provides for the recording of requests both to the British Library Document Supply Centre and those to other lending libraries; transmission of requests via ARTTel; receipt and loan of items; returns of items to their lending libraries; reminders; renewals and reports and statistics.

Descriptors — Inter-library loans

Operating System — MS DOS

Price Range — A

Languages — English

Reviews — Leeves, J., *A guide to inter-library loan management systems.* LINC, 1991.

MIRROR III

European Dealers/Distributors — Softklone (UK) Ltd

General Details — Mirror III is designed to reflect closely the features of the Crosstalk XVI communications package for the IBM and compatible PCs. It comes complete with a superset of the Crosstalk Script Language. This scripting capability and Mirror's background communications mode (call or answer) give the power to automate communications, and the freedom to perform other tasks on the PC. It includes a complete Prestel emulation, as well as many others, including DEC VT100/52, IBM 3101 and Televideo 910/920/925. File transfer protocols and Kermit, are supported, and there is a full screen Wordstar-like text editor.

Descriptors — Communications; Viewdata; Online search aid

Operating System — MS DOS

Price Range — A

Languages — English

Reviews — Dennis, T., Best comms software. *Which Computer (UK)*, March 1989, 46 - 56.
Clancy, S., Communications software for online searching on a PC. *ONLINE*, 14 (6), November 1990, 36 - 46.

MODIFILE, THE CONVENIENT CONVERTER

Supplier — Entity Software

European Dealers/Distributors — IOTA Consultancy (Netherlands); Euroscience (Netherlands)

General Details — ModiFile is a menu-driven program for the conversion of files, containing literature references from CD ROM (eg. SilverPlatter, Compact Cambridge, EBSCO, C.I.S), online (eg Datastar, Dialog, DIMDI) and disk (eg Current Contents). Once records have been converted by ModiFile, the files can be read into information retrieval programs such as Cardbox Plus, Pro-Cite and Scimate Manager.

Descriptors — Data reformatting

Operating System — MS DOS; DR DOS

Price Range — A

Languages — Dutch (Documentation and software); English (Software only)

Reviews — Micro-computer-programmatuur voor documentatie en bibliotheek - een softwarevergelijking voor conversie, opslag, ontsluiting en bibliotheekbeheer. VOGIN, The Hague, 1990.
Bleeker, A et al., Medline on CD-ROM; an evaluation after 6 months use. *Online Review*, 12 (4), 1988

MORPHS

Supplier — Rubber Consultants

General Details — MORPHS is an information retrieval system which supports numerical data and text. Commands or key words may be entered at any stage in the search. The main commands consist of a single character, and natural language makes the system comprehensible immediately. Help is provided automatically on the basis of elapsed inactive time. Cross referencing is built into the search routines. The system also permits browsing, the retention of compound word, and use of positional operators. Two systems of automatic indexing are available: a simple stoplist-based system and AIPIA — Artificial Intelligence Program for Automatic Indexing. There are several levels of document/user security so that confidential documents are fully protected. Abstracts are available online.

Descriptors — Information retrieval

Operating System — MS DOS

Price Range — C

Languages — English

MULTI ADAPTOR

Supplier — Inmagic Inc (US)

European Dealers/Distributors — Soutron Ltd (UK and Eire); EPMS bv (Netherlands)

General Details — MULTI Adaptor is a data reformatting package designed to convert data from a variety of formats into a format suitable for loading into the information retrieval package — INMAGIC Plus (see INMAGIC Plus). Data which can be converted includes field-tagged records from online databases; comma-delimited data (in ASCII) exported from many PC database and spreadsheet programs; and data transferred from one INMAGIC database to another (where the underlying data structure differs).

Descriptors — Data reformatting

Operating System — MS DOS

Price Range — A

Languages — English

MULTICOM

Supplier — Richard Cumming and Associates

General Details — Multicom provides access to 40 column viewdata services, and 80 column ASCII/VT100 services, such as electronic mail. The software features are controlled from a menu via the micro's function keys. Telephone numbers, with full log-on strings can be stored and dialled automatically. In viewdata mode, the help menu and display both appear on a split screen, or the display can occupy the full screen. Data can be saved to disc and recalled, both on and off line. A single keystroke switches Multicom to 80 column scrolling mode, in which data can be logged to a file, stored automatically and reviewed later. A screen editor allows off-line preparation of messages in viewdata mode, or messages can be prepared using a standard word processing package. Whether 40 or 80 columns, the display can easily be printed. More advanced features of Multicom include a telesoftware downloader/uploader, and an auto command facility. Many messages can be prepared prior to transmission, and a special protocol allows forms to be quickly completed off line with on-line selective transmission of fields. Incoming data can be converted to files suitable for use with a word processing program, without colour, graphics, etc. A mask can be made of a viewdata page so that all selected data is automatically lifted out. It can then be fed into standard letters, reports or files prepared on the word processor. A network version (Multicom Net)is available which operates on any PC Network using standard NETBIOS function calls. Modems can be attached to any PCs in the network, and shared by all others. An advanced version of Multicom (Multicom Plus) is also available.

Descriptors — Communications; Electronic mail; Online search aid; Viewdata

Operating System — MS DOS; OS/2; MS WINDOWS

Price Range — A

Languages — English

OASIS *

Supplier — Dawson Technology

General Details — OASIS is an integrated library housekeeping system developed by Dawson Technology (the software development subsidiary of Dawson Holdings plc the subscription agents) and incorporates Dawsons serials control system — SMS and the inter-library loans system — AIM (see OASIS-AIM and AIM 2). Functions offered are: catalogue and enquiry, circulation, acquisitions, serials control, inter-library loans. The full text retrieval package, Extract is also incorporated into the system. OASIS has clear, easy-to-follow screens with menu options always displayed along the bottom of the screen. It has multi-lingual facilities which allow entry of titles in European languages with full use of diacritical marks. For cataloguing purposes, data can be entered at the keyboard or online. Data from a wide variety of sources in MARC or structured non-MARC machine-readable formats can be accepted. Cataloguing functions include the presence of authority files for fields such as Author, Subject, Added Entry, Publisher and Series. For acquisitions, where Dawsons is used for subscriptions, an interface exists to enable orders to be sent to Dawsons electronically.

Descriptors — Integrated library housekeeping system; Cataloguing; OPAC; Information retrieval; Acquisitions; Online ordering; Circulation; Serials control; Inter-library loans

Operating System — MS DOS

Price Range — C

Languages — English

Reviews — An OASIS in the marketplace: the new system from Dawson Technology. *VINE*, 76, 1989.
The Integrated Workstation from Dawson Technology. *VINE*, 75, October, 1989.

OASIS-AIM *

Supplier — Dawson Technology

General Details — This inter-library loans system was originally developed by De Montfort University (formerly Leicester Polytechnic — see AIM-2). It was re-written when the Dawson's OASIS system was launched (see OASIS) and forms its inter-library loans module. OASIS-AIM can be bought along with the other library housekeeping modules of OASIS or it can be run independently. The system is menu-driven and offers facilities for managing, borrowing and lending items between libraries and with British Library Document Supply Centre.

Descriptors — Inter-library loans

Operating System — MS-DOS

Price Range — C

Languages — English

Reviews — Leeves, J., *A guide to inter-library loan management*. LINC, 1991. Marks, C., Inter-library lending packages: a review. *Library Micromation News*, 28, June 1990.

OASIS-SMS *

Supplier — Dawson Technology

General Details — Originally known as SMS (Serials Management System), this serials control system is now a module of the integrated library housekeeping system - OASIS (see OASIS). SMS can, however, be bought as a stand-alone system. It offers: check-in with claiming and routing slip functions; browse and enquiry on orders, reader/circulation and claim status; printing of orders to suppliers, reader analysis, fund/cost code analysis, and claims; online enquiry on title/publisher to the Dawson database, message service and electronic ordering and claiming; and total system security. Communication via PSS, SPNS or a private line is also possible. The system may be networked to provide a multi-user facility.

Descriptors — Online ordering; Serials control

Operating System — MS DOS

Price Range — C

Languages — English

OCLC CATALOGUING SOFTWARE

Supplier — OCLC Europe

General Details — OCLC (Online Computer Library Centre, Inc) is a non-profit membership organisation offering computer-based services to libraries, other educational organisations, and their users. OCLC provides one source for cataloguing, reference services, inter-library loan, union listing, and retrospective conversion. OCLC's database currently holds over 25 million bibliographic records. There are various PC-based software packages which work in conjunction with the OCLC database: the Cataloguing Micro Enhancer which saves time and money by producing and updating records in batch mode, editing bibliographical information offline, and exporting records to local systems; the ILL Micro Enhancer which processes inter-library loan requests offline; CAT CD450 Systems which use subsets of the Online Union Catalogue on compact disc to allow searching and editing offline; Passport Software, communications software for accessing OCLC online services and MICROCON which is an economic batch processing system for retrospective conversion.

Descriptors — Cataloguing; Inter-library loans; Communications; Data entry

Operating System — MS DOS

Languages — English

OCTOPUS *

Supplier — Mimu's

General Details — A cataloguing and library administration system.

Descriptors — Cataloguing

Operating System — MS DOS

ODYSSEY

European Dealers/Distributors — Shareware Marketing

General Details — Odyssey is a low cost communications package. It offers a wide range of terminal emulations, auto-dial and auto-logon together with uploading and downloading facilities. Features include support to MNP Level 5 in software; PASCAL-like fully compileable script language; full viewdata support (Prestel); VT 320 emulation; two text editors.

Descriptors — Communications; Downloading; Online search aid; Viewdata

Operating System — MS DOS

Price Range — A

Languages — English

Reviews — Blakeman, K., Low cost software: Odyssey 1.5 - A replacement for Procomm ? *IT LINK*, 5 (1), 1992, 4-6.
Gold, S., ProComm vs Odyssey. *PC World*, July 1989.

OMNIDOC/IMSOFT

Supplier — Integrated Documatics Ltd

General Details — OMNIDOC/IMSOFT is a documents management and image storage and retrieval package. The system manages documents providing facilities for document revisions, document distribution, reporting facilities, system administration and document circulation. The imaging facilities available include scanning control, storage optimisation, image manipulation and printing.

Descriptors — Records management; Image processing; Image retrieval

Operating System — MS DOS; UNIX

Languages — English

ONLINE SEARCH TUTOR JUNIOR (OST JUNIOR)

Supplier — Information Automation Ltd

General Details — The ONLINE SEARCH TUTOR is a complete self-training tool for anyone wishing to learn about searching the large bibliographic databases held by online search services such as the European Space Agency Information Retrieval Service (ESA-IRS). Its eight lessons feature pages of instruction in the skills of online searching, together with many examples and self-tests; demonstration searches; and simulations in which users must respond to the computer as if they were performing a real search. The ONLINE SEARCH TUTOR is aimed at anyone who will undertake bibliographic research. It expects no prior knowledge and so structures the learning process so that simple online searches can be conducted after a few hours work.

Descriptors — Computer aided learning; Training; Communications

Operating System — MS DOS

Price Range — A

Languages — English

OORNINKI *

Supplier — Henell Oy

General Details — No details supplied for this software package.

Operating System — MS DOS

OPACC

Supplier — Documedia Systems Ltd

General Details — OpAcc is an open-ended and portable information management system which utilises state of the art retrieval techniques to deliver improved access to information in any form. The system is designed to be independent of database, data format, operating system and hardware. All modules are discreet with well-defined interfaces and can be changed dynamically, thus making it easy for the system to be incrementally enhanced or replaced. Features include multi-media data entry, point and click editing of all formats; import of bibliographic records and full text documents; authority control and browsing enquiries; OPAC retrieval techniques (including relevance ranking and feedback, spelling correction, automatic stemming and combinatorial searching); document viewer with highlighting capability; and image storage and display. A typical OpAcc configuration runs with a Windows 3.1 front end and a local area network or Unix fileserver, its modularity allows a mix of Windows, X-Windows and character-based terminals to be used thus allowing users to work with their preferred interface and making use of existing equipment.

Descriptors — Information retrieval; Image retrieval

Operating System — MS DOS; MS WINDOWS; UNIX

Price Range — D/E

Languages — English

OPSYS *

Supplier — OPSYS

General Details — OPSYS is an integrated library housekeeping system running on mini and micro-computers. Its functions include cataloguing, loans, acquisitions, serials control, and statistics. The cataloguing module is MARC compatible and it is possible to have records in the same database in UNIMARC, INTERMARC and LCMARC formats. Authority controlled fields include: author, editor, collection, thesaurus, language and area of interest. The system is well designed for multi-media libraries and offers interfaces for end-user searching on terminals or minitels. Searchable fields include author, title, subject or collection. Right-hand truncation and Boolean operators can be used.

Descriptors — Integrated library housekeeping system; Cataloguing; OPAC; Circulation; Acquisitions; Serials control

Operating System — PICK; UNIX

Price Range — E (Hardware and software)

Languages — French

ORACLE LIBRARIES

Supplier — Oracle Corporation UK Ltd

General Details — Oracle Libraries (formerly known as Reflexion from Fretwell Downing) is a fully integrated library system based on the relational database ORACLE and incorporating the latest technological developments, such as open systems, hardware independence, and external interfaces, and which aims to be flexible enough to meet the different needs of different types of libraries. Oracle Libraries is modular in structure and comprises the following: cataloguing, circulation control, acquisitions, funds management, serials control, OPAC and management information and reporting. An inter-library loans module is planned. Oracle Libraries record formats reflect AACR2 criteria and UK MARC standards. Records can be both imported and exported in MARC format. Authority control is available for a wide range of fields.

Descriptors — Integrated library housekeeping system; Cataloguing; OPAC; Circulation; Acquisitions; Serials control

Operating System — UNIX

Special Hardware Requirements — Minimum hardware requirement — 486-based PCs

Price Range — E

Languages — English

Reviews — Fretwell-Downing's REFLEXION. *VINE*, 84, October 1991.

ORIEL

Supplier — The Advisory Unit for Microtechnology in Education

General Details — Software designed for information handling in a windows environment. Records can hold up to 80 fields and data entry is via a user-defined on-screen form. Search facilities include use of Boolean logic, nesting, right- and left-hand truncation, wild cards, range searching and string searching. Records can be displayed and printed in 2 standard formats together with a user-definable format. Records can also be printed in the form of address labels.

Descriptors — Information retrieval; School libraries

Operating System — MS WINDOWS

Special Hardware Requirements — MS WINDOWS

Price Range — A

Languages — English

PAPERBASE DE LUXE *

Supplier — Wight Scientific

General Details — PAPERbase De Luxe is a simple flat-file program designed specifically for the storing and manipulation of bibliographical data of the sort used by scientists and others writing referenced articles and reports, or by those simply wanting to keep track of their reading matter or offprints file.

Descriptors — Information retrieval; Personal bibliographic database; Reference management; Bibliographies

Operating System — MS DOS

Price Range — A

Languages — English

PAPRIKA *

Supplier — Decalog

General Details — Paprika provides integrated library housekeeping functions including cataloguing and retrieval, serials control and circulation control. The system has its own internal format with fields such as title, author, editor, year of publication, language, indexing terms etc. Up to 9 subject index terms can be assigned to each document, with access to a thesaurus. The exchange format used is UNIMARC. A variety of searching options allow for end-user searching and searching by the more experienced user.

Descriptors — Integrated library housekeeping system; Cataloguing; Circulation; Serials control

Operating System — MS DOS

Special Hardware Requirements — Minimum — IBM AT with 2 - 4 Mbytes of memory and a hard disk of at least 40 Mbytes

Price Range — D

Languages — French

PATCHWORK

Supplier — Chemdata S.A.; Chemdata Iberica S.A.; Chemdata Belgium

General Details — An electronic document management system

Descriptors — Image processing

Operating System — MS DOS

Languages — English; French

PC ANYWHERE

Supplier — Management Software Ltd

European Dealers/Distributors — Telesystems Ltd; Maxotex (France); PC Security (Norway)

General Details — PC ANYWHERE allows an unattended PC to be run from a remote location, using almost any personal computer or terminal. It will run all major software packages remotely, with complete access to printers and other peripherals (printing out at either location). Standard features include data compression for file transfer, using the ASCOM IV protocol, as well as error checking, and support for over 30 remote terminal types, including VT100 and Televideo 912. If communication is interrupted because of a line modem problem, the remote user can redial and continue work where it was left off, without losing data. The package includes software for the host PC, and for a PC at the remote end.

Descriptors — Communications; Remote access

Operating System — MS DOS

Price Range — A

Languages — English

PC INFO *

Supplier — DATACENTRALEN

General Details — No details supplied for this software package.

PC MASTER *

European Dealers/Distributors — Information und Kommunikation

General Details — The PC Master system utilises a common database for patents, trade marks and general legal matters. The modular design allows the user to start with any module and add others later. System features include online data entry and updating, interactive inquiry and record display. Multiple indexes allow browsing and direct access to selected files and data, and keyword searching. The system is menu driven and includes "help" screens. There is built-in multi-level security that limits individuals to authorised tasks only. A networking version is available.

Descriptors — Information retrieval

Operating System — MS DOS

Price Range — C/D

PC-ORDER/PC-ORDER PLUS/PC-QUERY

Supplier — B.H. Blackwell Ltd (Library Bookselling Division)

General Details — This suite of software allows libraries to take advantage of electronic ordering and communication without purchasing additional equipment or incurring expensive connect or transaction charges. With an IBM PC or compatible, a modem and Blackwell's PC-Order book ordering software, any library can order books electronically from Blackwell North America or from B.H.Blackwell Ltd. PC-Order transmits orders electronically to the Blackwell's; PC-Query provides order claiming and cancelling software that enhances the basic PC-Order system. PC-Order Plus provides a link between Blackwell North America's PC-Order and R.R.Bowker's CD-ROM based Books In Print Plus. It uses a single workstation equipped with BIP Plus which can be searched, a title located and the ISBN and bibliographic information brought to PC-Order's order entry files for transmission to Blackwell North America. PC-Order Plus also provides the link between PC-Order and Blackwell's PC-NTAS system.

Descriptors — Online ordering; Acquisitions; Communications

Operating System — MS DOS

Price Range — Free

Languages — English

PC STAIRS *

European Dealers/Distributors — D & R Software Services (Netherlands)

General Details — PC version of the Stairs information retrieval system.

Descriptors — Information retrieval

Operating System — MS DOS

PCTEX *

Supplier — Unina S.A.

General Details — PCTEX communications software comes with the PCTEX modem board. The software offers the following capabilities: Prestel, Teletel, CEPT, VT100,

IBM3101 and Bistel standards in 40 or 80 columns; screens saved to file or printed; screens retrieved from file; different character sets; 99 logon sequences, and an automatic run facility for demonstrations. DOS functions may be called from within PCTEX without loss of data or disconnecting from the host computer. New function keys may be defined, and there is a batch facility. File transfer facility is also available for Kermit, XMODEM, YMODEM, and NETBIOS MODEMS sharing script file facility.

Descriptors — Communications; Downloading; Viewdata

Operating System — MS DOS

PERSONAL LIBRARIAN

Supplier — Personal Library Software (US)

European Dealers/Distributors — Systematic Upgrade Computer Consultants Ltd(UK)

General Details — Personal Librarian (Version 3) is an advanced full text and retrieval system which can rapidly search large quantities of information. It was specifically designed to provide a host of powerful, interactive searching tools within a simple to use package. Experienced, occasional and novice searchers can retrieve significant details almost immediately. At the heart of a combination of user advisors is the expand function, which offers suggestions to help users word their enquiry to give the most productive results, often discovering unsuspected connections within a database. Results are relevance ranked in likely order of importance, with the most pertinent first which can be an advantage with large and complex information handling applications. Text can also be hypertext linked to text, data or images. It is possible to search and update databases simultaneously using the Concurrency feature. Windows Personal Librarian provides searching and display in WordPerfect and Word For Windows.

Descriptors — Image retrieval; Information retrieval; Thesaurus control; Hypertext

Operating System — MS DOS; MS WINDOWS; UNIX; APPLE OPERATING SYSTEM

Price Range — C

Languages — English

Reviews — *PC Magazine*, July 1992
Green, K., Personal Librarian at the Pilkington Technology Centre. *Library Micromation News*, December 1990.
New Law Journal, November 1990
Cisler, S., Personal Librarian and ROI: Personal Library Software's well-kept secrets. *Online*, 13 (4), July 1989, 120 - 122.
IT-LINK, 7, February 1989, 9
Computer and Libraries, December 1988, 2-3
Information World Review, September 1988, 16

PHOENIX LIBRARY & RESOURCE MANAGEMENT SYSTEM *

Supplier — Morgan Barnett Associates

General Details — Formerly known as the Easy Librarian (from Merlin Associates), this is a library cataloguing and lending system which runs on the Apple Macintosh and PCs under Windows. The underlying software is Omnis 5. The system is predominantly used in schools but is sufficiently flexible to be used in other environments. It makes good use of the intuitive approach in the Macintosh and Windows interface and is consequently easy to use. It is well suited to the transactional nature of loans due to its relational approach. This does, however, tend to fragment records making retrieval less powerful than in an indexed flat file database. Facilities are available for scanning in text and images.

Descriptors — Integrated library housekeeping system; Acquisitions; Cataloguing; Circulation; Image processing; School libraries

Operating System — APPLE OPERATING SYSTEM; MS WINDOWS

Price Range — A

Languages — English

PHOTOTRACER *

Supplier — Photofile Ltd

General Details — Phototracer is a retrieval system for picture libraries. It is a ready configured system with fixed length fields for title, keywords, location and notes. The keyword field is word indexed, other fields are string searched. A link with Geac's Picture Power to provide image display is under development.

Descriptors — Information retrieval; Image retrieval; Media control; Slide and photo management

Operating System — MS DOS

Price Range — A

Languages — English

Reviews — Bisco, A., Unlock the hidden treasure in photos. *Aslib Information*, 18 (9), Sept 1990, 280-284
Picture the future with Phototracer. *Library Micromation News*, 32, June 1991

PICTURE CARDBOX

Supplier — Business Simulations Ltd

European Dealers/Distributors — IOTA Consultancy (Netherlands)

General Details — Picture Cardbox is an information management and retrieval system combining the storage of high-quality images and text. It retains all of Cardbox-Plus's database functions for handling textual data and runs on any standard PC with a VGA screen (see Cardbox-Plus). No additional hardware, adaptor cards, or memory is required to store and display the images. Images can be captured using most scanners or frame-grabbers, and displayed alongside text, or, at the touch of a key, enlarged to fill the whole screen. A unique image compression and storage method ensures fast retrieval and minimises disk space required, making databases of many thousands of images feasible. It is available in single-user and multi-user (network) versions, and is an inexpensive but powerful picture database system. Applications include picture libraries, part and product catalogues, press cuttings, insurance inventories, signature verification, personnel and security databases.

Descriptors — Image processing; Image retrieval; Slide and photo management; Information retrieval

Operating System — MS DOS

Special Hardware Requirements — VGA screen

Price Range — B/C

Languages — English

Reviews — Ideal for exhibits. *Electronic Documents*, 1 (3), August 1992, 5.
A powerful and flexible graphical database. *BYTE*, 8, August 1991.
Cardbox-Plus update: pictures and a thesaurus. *Library Micromation News*, 33, September 1991, 2 - 6.

PICTURE FRAME

Supplier — Documedia Systems Ltd

General Details — Picture Frame adds colour or monochrome images onto almost any existing DOS-based PC application. Image references can be added anywhere in an application, with specific fields having to be defined, and the picture displayed at the touch of a button. Suggested uses include attaching photographs or video stills to records, adding images to a museum database, recording objects or paintings in an inventory database, identity pictures of users, embedding references to useful illustrations and diagrams in an abstract, adding a layout map to information screens. Picture Frame is fully compatible with both CALM and CLASS library management systems (see CALM and CLASS).

Descriptors — Image retrieval; Slide and photo management

Operating System — MS DOS

Price Range — A

Languages — English

POLYBASE/DIDEROT

Supplier — Polyphot

European Dealers/Distributors — Polyphot (UK) Ltd

General Details — POLYBASE is a general-purpose multi-media library software system for information and records management. DIDEROT automates loans, readers, acquisitions and other library housekeeping routines. Both feature user-defined data input screens, full indexing on all fields, search levels from novice to Boolean, keywords, thesaurus, external data capture, macro facilities, a variety of exit formats and password security. The system is used in a wide variety of organisations including commerce and industry, schools and colleges and local and central government.

Descriptors — Acquisitions; Cataloguing; Circulation; Integrated library housekeeping system; OPAC; School libraries

Operating System — MS DOS; UNIX

Price Range — B/C

Languages — French; English

Reviews — Ashworth, W., Polybase/Diderot. *New Library World*, 93, May 1992, 29-30. Database management software. *BYTE*, March, 1991.

PRETTYLIB *

Supplier — PrettyBit Softwares

General Details — No details supplied for this software package.

Operating System — MS DOS

PRO-CITE *

Supplier — Personal Bibliographic Software

General Details — Pro-Cite is a specialised database management system that enables the user to compile and maintain bibliographic information using 20 predefined and 6 user-defined document types, including books, journal articles, conference proceedings, manuscripts, and a variety of special media. It formats bibliographies according to ANSI, APA, Science Magazine or user-defined standards. Index terms can be assigned to each citation for full Boolean searching. Searching, sorting, and indexing is possible on all fields. Other features include: variable-length fields and records, detection of duplicates, a full-screen editor, and context sensitive help available at all times. A Pro-Cite database can contain up to 32,500 records. With the BIBLIO-LINK companion program (see also BIBLIO-LINK), the user can convert records downloaded from online databases to store and manipulate them in Pro-Cite. "Import", a Pro-Cite utility, converts word processing text files and records from other database programs into Pro-Cite format. Pro-Cite also scans word processing documents for abbreviated, in-text bibliographic references and produces a list of the complete citations by accessing the master Pro-Cite file. Pro-Cite is now directly compatible with ISI's "Current Contents on Diskette".

Descriptors — Personal bibliographic database; Bibliographies; Reference management; Information retrieval

Operating System — MS DOS; APPLE OPERATING SYSTEM

Price Range — A

Languages — English

Reviews — Busby, B., Pro-Cite in a special library. *Computers in libraries*, 10 (10), November 1990.

Cramer, M.D. and Markland, M.J., Newspaper indexing with Pro-Cite. *College & Research Libraries News*, 50 (9), October 1989.

Gabaldon, D.J., Bibliography managers save aggravation. *The Scientist*, 3 (19), October 1989.

Hanson, T., Pro-Cite and Bibliolinks. *Library Micromation News*, 26, December 1989.

Hanson, T.A. and Hanson, A.C., Managing bibliographies with Pro-Cite. *ASLIB Proceedings*, 41 (2), February 1989.

Joy, A.H., Using PBS' Biblio-Link programs for international/special databases. In *Computers in Libraries 1989. 4th annual conference and exhibition. Conference proceedings.* Meckler.

Mater, D.A., Pro-Cite: developing a statistical resources database. In *Computers in Libraries 1989. 4th annual conference and exhibition. Conference proceedings.* Meckler.

Nielsen, B., Doing your own software development: using tools on hand. *Database*, 12 (5).

PRO-SEARCH *

Supplier — Personal Bibliographic Software

General Details — Pro-Search can be used with a wide range of online host services as a means of storing host profiles, automatically logging on, uploading and downloading searches. For Dialog and BRS, the package can provide even more help. The "high level mode" features menus and prompts to guide a novice user through every step of constructing a search. For field-specific searches, an index window allows appropriate labels to be selected and transferred into the search. The package contains information about every Dialog and BRS database to help in database selection, and for those needing more details, the Dialog Bluesheets and BRS Aid-Pages can be displayed on the screen. For users who are familiar with either the Dialog or BRS search languages, Pro-Search allows them to search the other system using that language: Pro-Search translates the commands automatically. The Pro-Search accounting feature provides a means of keeping track of online charges.

Descriptors — Communications; Online search aid; Downloading

Operating System — MS DOS; APPLE OPERATING SYSTEM

Price Range — A

Languages — English

Reviews — Bjorner, S.N., In search of the ideal Macintosh search software. *Online*, 51, May 1991.
Moore, C., Pro-Search: easy access to Dialog, BRS and beyond. *Library Micromation News*, 26, December 1989.
Burg, B.A. and Tallent, E., The Searcher's Toolkit. *Information Technology and Libraries*, December 1988.

PROCOMM PLUS

European Dealers/Distributors — Shareware Publishing (European distributor)

General Details — ProComm Plus is an enhanced version of ProComm, one of the most popular shareware packages available. It is a fully featured, general purpose, communications package. A network version and a viewdata option are available. The system is easy to use with plenty of information on the screen, usually well laid out, making good use of windows and colours, and easy to follow. Most operations are controlled by mnemonic Alt key combinations and within the main operations there are often screen prompts to assist the user. ProComm Plus comes with a number of host profiles set up, mostly for bulletin board services. Profiles may be amended, deleted and an unlimited number of new ones set up. Autologon is provided by including each stage of the process in a script file which can be compiled in ProComm's own editor, PcEdit, or in external text editor or word processor. Logging on is initiated from DOS or from the dialling directory: automatic redial will continue indefinitely unless aborted by the user. Once online, the uploading features are limited for online searchers: files may be viewed before being transmitted but they can be sent only in block mode. Downloading features are flexible. A number of extra features are provided. For online searchers, the call monitoring is probably the most useful, allowing the number and duration of calls made to be logged.

Descriptors — Communications; Online search aid; Downloading

Operating System — MS DOS

Price Range — A

Languages — English; Spanish; French; German; Danish; Italian; Swedish; Dutch

Reviews — Ayre, R., Procomm continues to please. *PC Magazine*, April 1991, 20.
Clancy, S., Procomm Plus: the next generation of an excellent product. *Online*, 12 (5), September 1988, 70 - 73.
Hooked on comms. *PC Magazine (UK)*, 3 (10), October 1990, 54 - 76.
Blakeman, K., Software Review - ProComm Plus Version 2.0. *UKOLUG Newsletter*, 2 (5), September/October 1991.
Erdt, T., ProComm 4.2.2 software review. *Comput. Humanit. (Netherlands)*, 23 (2), April 1989.
A comparative review of communications packages. *Computers in Libraries*, 2 (10), June 1989.
Gold, S., ProComm vs Odyssey. *PC World*, July 1989.
Jackson, P., Online software. *PC World Focus*, September 1989.
Nielson, B., Using ProComm Scripts, uploading your mail, and other helpful hints. *Online*, 14 (2), March 1990.
Robertson, M., Quick-start Procomm scripts. *PC World*, 7 (10), October 1989.
Tsaousidis, S., Procomm Plus versus Telix 3.0: the duel of the communication giants. *Micro (Germany)*, 1, January 1989.

PROGEN LIBRARY *

Supplier — Limrose Software Ltd

General Details — Progen Library offers cataloguing and circulation facilities. Items may be retrieved by title, author, publisher, publication date, ISBN and keywords. Keywords can be entered in any order and combined together for more complex searches. Progen Library is suitable for libraries with about 100,000 books. The package also produces overdue notices and provides "borrower traps". A report writer will produce reports as well as printing catalogue lists and spine labels.

Descriptors — Cataloguing; Circulation

Operating System — MS DOS

Price Range — A/B

Languages — English

Q-CAL

Supplier — Information Automation Ltd

General Details — q-CAL is a training package which, without taking its users online, teaches the skills of online searching on the Questel databases. Using traditional Computer Assisted Learning (CAL) techniques, q-CAL introduces users to the commands necessary for searching the databases on Questel. q-CAL is a self-contained package which first instructs and then simulates the Questel software as trainees try out the commands they have been taught as if performing a real search online. Users are shown how to connect to Questel, choose a database, search, display and print records, and end a session. The search instruction includes the use of truncation, proximity operators, Boolean operators, and numerical operators.

Descriptors — Computer aided learning; Training; Communications

Operating System — MS DOS

Price Range — A

Languages — English

QUEST

Supplier — The Advisory Unit for Microtechnology in Education

General Details — An educational information handling program which allows the user to set up a database with up to 80 fields, edit existing databases and then to interpret them. The data may be interrogated in both simple and complex ways, and selected information displayed on screen or sent to a printer in two different formats. There are a number of built-in facilities which enable the data to be sorted and justified, and utilities are available which allow data to be displayed as a bar chart or scatter diagram. Address labels may be produced and more flexible editing facilities are also offered by these utilities. QUEST is available in a number of formats for both BBC and RML computers as well as IBM PCs and compatibles. In all cases, some utilities and sample databases are included.

Descriptors — Information retrieval; School libraries

Operating System — MS DOS; RISC OS

Price Range — A

Languages — English

RAIZ *

Supplier — Swisstar Software

General Details — RAIZ is a conversion program that can convert downloaded data from the host DIMDI into formats that can be loaded into local database programs.

Descriptors — Data reformatting

Operating System — MS DOS

Languages — Dutch

RASMUS

Supplier — Cambridge Software

General Details — RASMUS is a personal reference management system. The user must set up a thesaurus of keywords and each keyword may have attached to it any number of associated keywords or subkeys. A precis must be made of all papers, bibliographies etc., and occurrences of keywords underlined. The user's precis of an original document equates to an "abstract". All database records, or "abstracts" are of variable length, and there is no limit to database, record, keyword and associated keyword length. Reports may be generated. Facilities allow the sorting of selected abstracts, and the printing of letters. There is a series of communications utilities to connect to remote computers and download information.

Descriptors — Personal bibliographic database; Bibliographies; Reference management; Communications; Information retrieval

Operating System — MS DOS

Price Range — A

Languages — English

RC-LIB *

Supplier — ICL DATA A/S

General Details — No details supplied for this software package.

REACHOUT

European Dealers/Distributors — Telesystems Ltd

General Details — Reachout allows a PC to take control of another PC in another location and run applications including Windows. Files may be transferred in either direction. Auto dial/auto answer modems are fully supported.

Descriptors — Communications; Remote access

Operating System — MS DOS

Price Range — A

Languages — English

RECALL PLUS

Supplier — Insoft Ltd (UK and Europe)

General Details — A powerful information retrieval system capable of searching up to 65,000 documents simultaneously. Unlike conventional database management systems, Recall Plus requires no pre-definition of keywords or "fields" and no artificial structuring of information (although it is also capable of handling structured information). Instead it takes the contents of existing text or word processor files and automatically builds an index of every word or number it encounters. Features include stem searching, phrase searching and synonym searching together with a user-definable thesaurus. A full range of Boolean operators are supported together with word proximity commands, bracketing, "sounds like", wildcards, and synonyms. Comprehensive browsing facilities are provided and the system is fully menu-driven. Recall also incorporates optional advanced features including full image support and hypertext linking. A network version is also available.

Descriptors — Information retrieval; Thesaurus control; File indexing; Free text retrieval; Image retrieval; Hypertext

Operating System — MS DOS; MS WINDOWS

Price Range — A/B

Languages — English

Reviews — *PC Magazine*, July 1992

RECORDS MANAGEMENT SYSTEM *

European Dealers/Distributors — MFT Computer Systems Ltd

General Details — Records Management System is a computer-based system which provides a means of simplifying and speeding up the monitoring of the movements of files or folders within a large organisation. Access to information is from a wide variety of viewpoints and the system incorporates sophisticated searching and reporting facilities.

Descriptors — Archives; Records management

Operating System — UNIX

Languages — English

RED RYDER *

Supplier — Public Domain

General Details — Red Ryder is a full-featured, general-purpose communications program with a comprehensive scripting language. Emulations include TTY, VT52 and VT102. Scroll controls and communications parameters are in the form of icons to be clicked by the mouse and screen archiving and printing are similarly controlled. Logon information can be stored and macros can be defined. The last shareware version of Red Ryder was 9.4. It has since been released commercially under the name: White Knight.

Descriptors — Communications

Operating System — APPLE OPERATING SYSTEM

Price Range — Public Domain

Languages — English

Reviews — Noble, I., Public domain communications software for the Apple Macintosh. *Library Micromation News*, 29, September 1990.

REFERENCE MANAGER *

Supplier — Research Information Systems Inc (US)

European Dealers/Distributors — Silverplatter Information Ltd (UK); DOC 6 (Spain); Bilaney Consultants GmbH (Germany); Bilaney Consultants Ltd (UK)

General Details — A microcomputer-based software package developed to manage selected references for quick retrieval and bibliography generation. Reference Manager is menu-driven, and interfaces with a variety of word processing packages. The package assumes standard bibliographical input and thus provides ready to use data structures for journal articles, books, chapters in books, abstracts, unpublished papers and in-press references. Indexes are created automatically for fields such as author, editors, keywords, journal and year of publication and a synonym table is available for journal names. Downloaded records from certain databases can be reformatted and imported into the system using an optional "Capture" program. Records can also be imported directly from "Reference Update", a subscription service which provides a weekly update on diskette on the latest publications in biology and medicine. Searching is very structured and facilities include use of Boolean logic, nesting, word adjacency, right-hand truncation, index browsing and range searching. Powerful report format capabilities mean that Reference Manager can prepare bibliographies in virtually any journal style.

Descriptors — Personal bibliographic database; Bibliographies; Reference management; Information retrieval

Operating System — MS DOS; APPLE OPERATING SYSTEM

Price Range — A

Languages — English

Reviews — Gabaldon, D.J., Bibliography managers save aggravation. *The Scientist*, 3 (19), October 1989.
Hanson, T., The Reference Manager bibliographic software package. *Library Micromation News*, 25, September 1989.
Matus, N. and Beutler, E.B., Reference Update and Reference Manager: Personal computer programs for locating and managing references. *BioTechniques*, 7 (6).

REFSYS SUPER

Supplier — BIOSOFT

General Details — Refsys Super is designed to store bibliographic references and to provide a means of recalling and printing selected lists of the references in specified formats. It therefore enables the user to create his own database of literature references which are cited most frequently. Refsys Super also provides a means of cross-referencing the references by subject categories, of searching the database for any term and of searching manuscripts for citations from which a bibliography can automatically be prepared. The program can import references from databases such as Medline or from pre-existing bibliographies.

Descriptors — Information retrieval; Personal bibliographic database; Reference management

Operating System — MS DOS

Price Range — A

Languages — English

REFWRITER

Supplier — Jackson Smith Associates (UK)

European Dealers/Distributors — Information Automation Ltd (UK); EPMS bv (Netherlands)

General Details — RefWriter is a data conversion package that can be used to reformat un-edited, downloaded data. User-defined templates control the conversion and once a template has been developed it can be used every time online data is downloaded. RefWriter has facilities for extracting, re-ordering or excluding data elements, and output may be enhanced by user-defined text, automatic reference numbering and user-supplied field labels. Items may be viewed during conversion to sift out those not required. There is also a utility which can be used to analyse the tagged fields in a downloaded file as an aid to setting up the template.

Descriptors — Data reformatting

Operating System — MS DOS

Price Range — A

Languages — English

RELAY GOLD

European Dealers/Distributors — Softkey (Netherlands); Comware International Ltd (UK and Europe)

General Details — A communications package specifically written for file transmission and terminal emulation on the IBM PC. Terminals supported include VT52, VT100, VT220, VT240 with Regis graphics and IBM 3179/8 models 2 - 5 with graphics. Connections supported include ASYNCH, GATEWAY, COAX, INT-14 and TOKEN RING. Host parameter files can be set up and uploading and downloading can be performed at the same time. A network version (LAN) is also available.

Descriptors — Communications; Downloading

Operating System — MS DOS; MS WINDOWS

Languages — English

SABINI

Supplier — Automatiacion de Bibliotecas

European Dealers/Distributors — DOC 6 (Spain)

General Details — SABINI is an integrated local library system which supports library functions using MARC format for bibliographic description. The acquisitions subsystem integrates with the bibliographic database and offers financial control and the ability to set up a supplier file. A thesaurus and authority module is available for use with the catalogue. The catalogue database may be searched using Boolean logic. "Select", "combine" and "limit" commands are available, and both right-hand and left-hand truncation are supported. Various output formats are permitted to either paper, microform or magnetic tape. A circulation module is available. The system also runs minis and mainframes under the name SABINA. It is the system with most installations in Spain.

Descriptors — Integrated library housekeeping system; Cataloguing; Information retrieval; Circulation; Thesaurus control

Operating System — PICK; UNIX

Price Range — E

Languages — Spanish; Catalan; English

SAILS *

Supplier — Swets & Zeitlinger bv

European Dealers/Distributors — Swets UK Ltd; Europériodiques - Swets France

General Details — SAILS is a serials control system developed by the subscriptions agents Swets & Zeitlinger.

Descriptors — Serials control

Operating System — MS DOS

Languages — Dutch; English; French

SALBIN PC *

Supplier — Edinburgh University Library

General Details — SALBIN PC was developed by the Scottish Academic Libraries Network (SALBIN) and is a simple communications package for use over JANET (the Joint Academic Network — UK) enabling library users to look up other academic libraries'

catalogues for themselves, and record the results of their search in print or on their own floppy disk. There are two versions: the User's version which aims to be as simple and friendly as possible and the Professional version which allows for local tailoring and maintenance.

Descriptors — Communications; Downloading

Operating System — MS DOS

Price Range — A

Languages — English

Reviews — Ralls, M., SALBIN. *IT's News*, 24, July 1991.
Ralls, M. SALBIN. *VINE*, 75, October 1989.

SEARCHMAGIC

Supplier — Inmagic Inc (US)

European Dealers/Distributors — Soutron Ltd (UK and Eire); EPMS bv (Netherlands); LIS (Netherlands); DOC 6 (Spain)

General Details — SearchMAGIC is a stand-alone, search-only version of INMAGIC to be used with any database created with INMAGIC Plus (see INMAGIC Plus). SearchMAGIC is designed for occasional or novice users and provides a simple searching interface. At the touch of a key it is possible to: search many fields at once; choose search terms from a browse list; display the words or terms in any search field, and then paste them into the search request; examine any record in detail; display searches in a variety of formats; press another key to remove the record from the search; display and print formatted reports (you do not have to remember format names — SearchMAGIC automatically presents information in a pre-selected style); jump to full INMAGIC command-driven searching to use INMAGIC's Boolean commands for more complex searches. SearchMAGIC is also available in locked form for licensed database publication (eg on CD-ROM).

Descriptors — Information retrieval; OPAC; CD-ROM interface

Operating System — MS DOS; VMS

Price Range — A

Languages — English; Spanish; Dutch

SGBC *

Supplier — Logitec Informatica

General Details — SGBC is an integrated library management system written in Clipper. It is compatible with IBERMARC and offers modules for cataloguing and enquiry, acquisitions, circulation and serials control. The system also has a CD-ROM interface and generates statistics for each of its basic modules.

Descriptors — Integrated library housekeeping system; Cataloguing; Acquisitions; Circulation; Serials control

Operating System — MS DOS

Price Range — C

Languages — Spanish

SHERLOCK *

European Dealers/Distributors — FIZ Technik e.V.

General Details — Sherlock aims to help online database users to find the information they need without prior knowledge of the databases available. Entering German language keywords provides a list of suggested databases to search; then "Search Cards" enable query by forms, with the system adjusting the template according to the particular file and fields concerned.

Descriptors — Online search aid

Operating System — MS DOS

Languages — German

SIDETALK *

Supplier — OVM Sopiana Ltd

General Details — An interface which cuts out the need to learn host command languages. Front ends have been developed for Pergamon, Dialog and Datastar. SIDETALK runs concurrently with other programs and has an extensive call-logging capability which will show you how much time you have spent on the host.

Descriptors — Online search aid

Operating System — MS DOS

Languages — English

SIMS LIBRARY MANAGEMENT MODULE

Supplier — SIMS Ltd

General Details — SIMS Ltd produce software for schools administration and include a module for the management of the school library. This modular approach allows the Library module either to stand alone or to be integrated into the whole SIMS system allowing borrower details to be taken and regularly updated from existing staff and pupil data files. A barcode reader can be used for fast entry of data for routine tasks eg. issuing, returning, reservations. Extensive search facilities, both by single and multiple fields, are available. In addition fast entry from lists and wildcard entries on a number of fields including keywords are available for catalogue entry and for searches. Some customisation is allowed by the user eg. codes allowing recording of various types of resource, availability and time/number limitations. Security is provided by several user levels, ID and password with system securities through SIMS System Manager. A wide range of standard reports and analyses can be produced through the system.

Descriptors — Integrated library housekeeping system; Cataloguing; Circulation; School libraries

Operating System — MS DOS

Price Range — B

Languages — English

SMARTCOM II *

Supplier — Hayes Microcomputer Products Inc

General Details — SMARTCOM II provides error-free communications with Hayes verification and XMODEM protocols. It is possible to record up to 25 messages, files or letters at a time and transmit them at night when phone rates are low. The software stores telephone numbers, log on procedures and communications protocols which can be later executed with a few keystrokes. Other features include: on-screen password protection; data capture at the press of a key; the printing of data while recording it to disk; voice to data transmission, and the emulation of DEC VT100 and VT52 terminals.

Descriptors — Communications; Online search aid; Downloading

Operating System — MS DOS; APPLE OPERATING SYSTEM

Special Hardware Requirements — Hayes smartmodem

Languages — English

Reviews — Bjorner, S.N., In search of the ideal Macintosh search software. *ONLINE*, 51, May 1991.

SMARTCOM III *

Supplier — Hayes Microcomputer Products Inc

General Details — Powerful, general-purpose communications software. Provides automatic logon, downloading to disk, saving to retrieve buffer of limited (100K) size for transfer to disk or printer, and complicated uploading of search strategies. Allows transfer of autologon macros from Smartcom II. Provision to "learn" scripts for autologon and repetitive online operations. Supports 2400 baud online searching and allows two simultaneous communication sessions. Supports Kermit, XMODEM, XMODEM CRC, YMODEM, emulates VT100 and VT102 and supports remote access.

Descriptors — Communications

Operating System — MS DOS

Price Range — A

Languages — English

Reviews — Koga, J.S., Smartcom III: A powerful, flexible program ... but not designed for online searching. *Database*, 11, (2), 1988, 109-115
Dennis, T., Best comms software. *Which Computer*, March 1989.

SMARTERM *

Supplier — P&P Micro Distributors Ltd

General Details — SMARTERM 220 combines terminal emulation and text and data file transfer capabilities in a single software package. Full functionality of the PC is retained while communicating with the host system as a VT220, VT102, VT100, VT52, or TTY terminal. SMARTERM also has the ability to define eight separate setup configurations, and "smart" softkeys to simplify auto-dial, log-in, file transfer, and other frequently-performed tasks. The file transfer functions of SMARTERM include downloading to a disk file and uploading of text and binary program or data files to the host computer without special programming. SMARTERM also includes the ability to transmit and receive files using a choice of three error-free protocols: XMODEM, KERMIT, and Persoft's own PDIP protocol.

Descriptors — Communications; Downloading

Operating System — MS DOS

Languages — English

SOD

European Dealers/Distributors — DOC 6 (Spain)

General Details — SOD is a housekeeping system designed to handle inter-library loans and document supply requests as well as related administrative and statistical functions. Its major features are: management of user information, lending/borrowing and supplying/purchasing procedures, payments/invoicing, usage statistics, IFLA request forms, e-mail. The program can be customised for local needs and runs on LANs.

Descriptors — Inter-library loans

Operating System — MS DOS

Price Range — C

Languages — Spanish

SONAR

Supplier — Virginia Systems (Canada)

European Dealers/Distributors — MSC Information Retrieval Technologies

General Details — Sonar is free-text retrieval software designed for researching and annotating large bodies of text. Its powerful text retrieval functions all users to search through many documents at a time with accuracy and speed.

Descriptors — Information retrieval; File indexing

Operating System — MS WINDOWS; APPLE OPERATING SYSTEM

Price Range — A

Languages — English

Reviews — Côté, R. and Diehl, S., Searching for common threads. *BYTE*, June 1992.

SOUTRON LIBRARY SYSTEM

Supplier — Soutron Ltd

General Details — The Soutron Library System (formerly the Sydney Library System) is a library and information management system with modules for cataloguing and enquiry, acquisitions, circulation, serials management and a MARC record interface. The system is menu-driven throughout providing a consistent interface for users. The cataloguing module (the "Base System") is the heart of the system and is used to build and maintain the database used by the other modules. It offers authority control for the maintenance of controlled indexing terms including cross references (such as SEE, SEE ALSO, BROADER & NARROWER TERM) and will print catalogues, reports and labels. To build up the catalogue, records can be converted from existing machine-readable sources including records in MARC format (using the MARC Communications Interface Module) or keyed in with real-time updating. Acquisitions includes: pre-order searching, online supplier file; currency conversion, fund accounting; normal, temporary and standing orders and claiming. The issue system caters for a barcode reader, reservations, overdues, borrower traps and management reports. The serials module maintains a subscription file, and enables journal check-in, claims, invoice processing and report generation. Online links to serials subscription agencies are under development. The system can be single-user or networked. A Report Writer is available with the system for user-defined report generation.

Descriptors — Integrated library housekeeping system; Cataloguing; OPAC; Acquisitions; Circulation; Serials control; MARC Interface

Operating System — MS DOS; DR DOS; UNIX; VMS

Price Range — C

Languages — English

STAR

Supplier — Cuadra Associates Inc (US)

European Dealers/Distributors — Omegon Computersystemen bv (Netherlands); Abacus Software Ltd (UK); Dark Star Information Systems (UK); Sweetens Computer Services (UK); Glomas Deutschland GmbH; MCPS S.A. (Belgium); Nimo Data AB (Sweden)

General Details — STAR is a multi-user integrated text management and information/image retrieval software package designed for descriptive information management without programmer support. STAR provides the built-in features needed for managing and using text databases: variable length fields and records; validation and authority file control; import/export facilities; high performance retrieval with end-user interfaces (for both experienced and novice searchers: menu- and command-driven); thesaurus support; many options for reports. Applications can be defined by the user, while pre-defined applications are also available.

Descriptors — Database management; Information retrieval; Image retrieval

Operating System — AMOS (Alpha Micro Operating System); UNIX

Price Range — C

Languages — English

Reviews — *Bull Med. Libr. Assoc.* 79 (2), 1991, 189-194
Information Services & Use, 10, 1990, 381-390

STATUS/PC *

Supplier — Harwell Computer Power Ltd

European Dealers/Distributors — Status/PC is available worldwide - contact Harwell Computer Power (UK) for up-to-date details of European distributors.

General Details — Status/PC is the microcomputer version of Status which was developed by the UK Atomic Energy Authority to handle both full text and structured text information. Status forms the basis of various configured systems: Status/M for museum collections; Legal Know-How for lawyers; and CORA, a document management system. Images and bar codes can be linked to Status applications and it has also been used for CD-ROM applications. Status can be used in its original command-based mode, or through a series of question and display panels. Menu-driven searching, help functions and often-used routines can be set up in the system using "macros". Records (called "articles") are made up of "keyed fields" which contain numeric or value information, and "named sections" for textual information. There are no limits on record or field size. Data entry is in batch mode from many different sources or from the keyboard within Status. Search facilities include general browsing, word and phrase searching, truncation and wild card, Boolean logic, field and range searching, and proximity searching which is valuable for long passages of text. Unindexed data may be searched by means of a text scan. Data output can be defined using formats designed by the user. A new version of Status/PC incorporating greater functionality is under development.

Descriptors — Information retrieval; Thesaurus control; Free text retrieval

Operating System — MS DOS

Price Range — C

Languages — English

Reviews — Bain, M. et al., *Free text retrieval systems: a review and evaluation.* London: Taylor Graham, 1989.

Bryant, G., Banking on Status. *Information World Review*, July 1989.

STN EXPRESS

Supplier — STN International

European Dealers/Distributors — Royal Society of Chemistry (UK); Compagnie d'Application et d'Assistance en Documentation (CAPADOC) (France); Cobidoc bv (Netherlands); IDC-KTHB (Sweden and Finland)

General Details — STN EXPRESS is a communications package which combines communications with chemical structure building. The configurations of five online hosts (CAS Online, BIOSIS Previews, Compendex, Phys, Inspec) can be prestored or the package can be used as a teletype terminal emulator by sending instructions manually. Both text and structures can be built offline and later uploaded to an STN file. Text and graphics can be captured to a file and the special features of graphic handling in STN EXPRESS means that enhanced printouts and reports can be produced in a variety of formats. All the advanced facilities to be expected of a communications package are available eg: typing ahead, editing a line, scrolling back through previous command lines etc.

Descriptors — Communications; Online search aid; Chemical information

Operating System — MS DOS; MS WINDOWS; APPLE OPERATING SYSTEM

Price Range — A

Languages — English

STN PERSONAL FILE SYSTEM

Supplier — STN International

General Details — The STN Personal File System was developed by Fachinformationszentrum (FIZ) Karlsruhe and Kramer & Hofmann, Saarbrucken. It is a combination of a powerful retrieval system and a data pre- and postprocessing system. It is designed to meet the requirements of scientists and other users who need a text retrieval system which can handle input from various sources. The retrieval language uses similar commands to the Messenger retrieval system used by the online system —

STN International and includes use of Boolean and proximity operators. Database structures are flexible and can be set up manually where the pre-defined structures supplied are not appropriate. Up to 32,000 records can be held in each database, each with up to 200 fields and any number of subfields. Very complex Personal Files, including sophisticated input/edit screens, can be created by using the Programmer's Guide which is available on request in German and English.

Descriptors — Information retrieval; Reference management; Personal bibliographic database

Operating System — MS DOS

Special Hardware Requirements — MS DOS version 3.3 or higher

Price Range — C

Languages — English; German

Reviews — Opbouwen van eigen databases: STN Personal File System. Nieuws *Berichten Informatie (Cobidoc bv)*, 8 (61), 1991.
Hanson, T., The STN Personal File System. *Library Micromation News*, 33, September 1991.

STRIDE

Supplier — BNF-Fulmer

European Dealers/Distributors — Samsom Veldkamp bv

General Details — STRIDE is a powerful and versatile thesaurus management system which builds and maintains standard vocabularies which may then be used during information indexing and retrieval. All the main ISO 2788 and ANSI A39.19 relationships and display formats may be used and users can also readily define other special relationships and display formats. Hypertext facilities enable the user to shift to related contexts while scanning a thesaurus. STRIDE allows both interactive and batch editing and has facilities for automatic logging of transactions. All modifications are carried out in real time. STRIDE has been interfaced to the free-text information retrieval system - Status (see Status/PC).

Descriptors — Thesaurus control

Operating System — MS DOS; UNIX; MS WINDOWS

Price Range — B

Languages — English

Reviews — *Database*, 13 (6), December 1990.

STRIX

European Dealers/Distributors — D.R.F. Van Bremen Informatica Advies bv (Netherlands); Business File Ltd (Europe other than Netherlands)

General Details — Strix provides the facility to create one or more textual databases, each with its own structure defined by the user. An unlimited number of databases can be set up with up to 50 fields and 32,000 characters per record. Data can be entered either directly from word processors, other software or scanners, editing of the data is possible. Records are added to the system and partially indexed in real time but full indexing has to be carried out in batch mode. Strix facilities include word or phrase (non-linked phrases are "string searched"), truncation with wild card letters or strings, Boolean logic (including the "exclusive or" operator), field searching, range and proximity searching. Search results may be displayed to screen or printer. Strix can be driven from a command line or a form fill interface which allows individual users forms for data entry, searching, display and a report generator for printing. Strix can be linked to library management software and image management software.

Descriptors — Information retrieval

Operating System — MS DOS; UNIX

Price Range — B/C

Languages — English; Dutch

Reviews — Parfitt, Y., First impressions of Strix on a IBM PS/2 Model 60. *Computers & Libraries*, 2 (4), November 1988.
Tucker, G., The STRIX system in HTV Film Library. *Audiovisual Librarian*, 14(2), May 1988.

SUPERCOM *

Supplier — Communicator Software Engineering bv

General Details — SUPERCOM is a simple, inexpensive program suitable for online information retrieval and downloading.

Descriptors — Communications; Downloading

Operating System — MS DOS

Languages — Dutch

SUPERDOC *

Supplier — AIDEL

General Details — SUPERDOC is an information retrieval system which includes facilities for searching by keywords, loans control using barcodes if required, production of a variety of printed output etc. It can interface with optical disks and can be used with audio-visual peripherals such as videodisks.

Descriptors — Information retrieval; Archives

Operating System — MS DOS

Price Range — C

Languages — French

SUPERFILE *

Supplier — Southdata Ltd

European Dealers/Distributors — Imago Logica

General Details — A database management system without its own applications-generating language — code is written in the standard language (eg Pascal). Searching is sophisticated with features such as use of Boolean logic, nesting, word adjacency, truncation, wild cards, range searching, index browsing, etc. Data is input via screen forms or imported in machine readable form. Display and printed outputs are user-definable. A new very large database system (Superfile VLDB) is available with full-text indexing. Databases are compatible with ordinary Superfile products, but are currently read-only. A BATCH UPDATE facility exists for updating all records in a Superfile database which conform to a user-defined model. (See also Convert and Colossus.)

Descriptors — Information retrieval

Operating System — MS DOS; UNIX; VMS

Price Range — A

Languages — English

Reviews — Heaton, C., Superfile and Colossus in Cambridgeshire Libraries. *Library Micromation News*, 27, March 1990.

SWISSTAR *

Supplier — Swisstar Software

General Details — SWISSTAR is specially designed for the conversion of common bibliographic formats which can be downloaded from online host computers and CD-ROM, into another ASCII format to be imported by the users' database management systems. The raw material that has been downloaded can be used as a valid input file for SWISSTAR without any editing. One can easily define new conversions, with a maximum of 89 fields. The conversion definition files are questionnaires in ASCII format, that are filled in with a wordprocessor. SWISSTAR permits "Find and Replace" operations defined at field level, as well as replacing characters by new labels (field splitting). SWISSTAR can operate batch files, accepting parameters in the command line and giving control back to MS DOS when conversion is completed. SWISSTAR comes with conversion definition files for DIMDI, DIALOG tagged format, ESA download format, DATASTAR, EBSCO and COMPACT CAMBRIDGE Medline, Current Contents on Floppy, and STN to a Cardbox-Plus external format. They can easily be modified for database systems like Inmagic, Freebase or Superfile. SWISSTAR can print an online search while underlining the search terms. English and Dutch versions available.

Descriptors — Data reformatting

Operating System — MS DOS

Price Range — A

Languages — Dutch; English

Reviews — Sieverts, E.G., Software for conversion of downloaded data; criteria for comparison and assessment. In: *Online Information 89; 13th International Online Information Meeting*. Oxford: Learned Information, 1989.

SYLLABUS

European Dealers/Distributors — Documedia Systems Ltd

General Details — Syllabus is a complete learning resource control system which enables local education authorities to provide a better schools library service or educational resource centre. Syllabus controls everything relating to managing resources, both material and intellectual, including cataloguing, booking, stock and loan control of stock, delivery and collection. Fund accounting, invoicing and management reporting are also fully supported. Syllabus comprises the following modules : delivery and collection; invoicing; report generator; import/export. Because Syllabus is written in Oracle, a wide range of hardware platforms are available, enabling Syllabus to fit in with existing policies and preferences on hardware.

Descriptors — Resource control; School libraries

Operating System — MS DOS; UNIX

Price Range — D/E

Languages — English

SYNOPSYS *

Supplier — Genesys Software-vertriebs GmbH

General Details — SYNOPSYS is a software tool for processing the results of online database searches automatically. SYNOPSYS eliminates all unnecessary host information and sorts retrieved items on any user-specified fields. It identifies duplicate items in one or more files. It extracts fields from retrieved items and strings them together with their context. Strings can be marked on the screen and on the printer. SYNOPSYS is able to recognise the formats of the most important retrieval languages, other formats can be defined individually. SYNOPSYS comes with a built-in editor which is used for the screening and editing of all text files. Production of printed output is straightforward.

Descriptors — Data reformatting

Operating System — MS DOS

Price Range — B

TAMIL

Supplier — Tamil

General Details — TAMIL is a cataloguing and retrieval system designed for documentation centres and libraries which possess from 5,000 to 200,000 documents. Functions available include cataloguing, circulation and serials control. Record lengths are variable with a maximum record length of 3,200 characters. The system supports up to 200,000 records with 100 fields per record. Editing facilities are available. The software allows

Boolean searching, numerical searching, search term truncation, field-based and full text searching, nested search terms, alternative query languages and synonyms. A print generator is available. A thesaurus with the relations BT/NT/SA/USE/USF/NOTES is present and is used during input and retrieval. The serials subsystem offers: ordering, receiving, claiming, and editing facilities: circulation slips (up to 9 lists of 9 users per copy of one issue), serials catalogues sorted by vendors, titles, readers, etc.

Descriptors — Cataloguing; Information retrieval; Circulation; Serials control; Thesaurus control

Operating System — MS DOS; UNIX; VMS

Price Range — C/D

Languages — French; English; Spanish

Reviews — Demians, G.F.J., TAMIL, Gestion des prêts, Télédéchargement et Thésaurus. *IDT 87, Textes et Communications* ADBS/ANRT, 1987.

TELEPEN LIBRARY SYSTEM *

Supplier — S B Electronic Systems Ltd

General Details — The Telepen Library System provides circulation control, reservation handling and lists all overdues and recalls. It holds on-line an up-to-date record of all current readers, loans and reservation transactions and traps reserved books when they are returned. It restricts borrowing by readers attempting to exceed their allotted quota and indicates overdue books when they are returned. It traps books and readers designated as "hot". It is possible to find out which books are loaned to a particular reader and which reader has a particular book and several categories of books and readers are handled. Fail safe procedures allow continued operation after a System fault and system controls can be overridden by library staff.

Descriptors — Circulation

Operating System — MS DOS

Special Hardware Requirements — System 550 AT compatible workstation with RAM disk; 2 Mb RAM disk, 'Link' software for multi-user.

Price Range — C

Languages — English

TELETEL EMULATOR DISK

Supplier — Coralplan Ltd

General Details — Teletel is the French national videotext system accessible in France via a Minitel terminal and a telephone line. This Teletel Emulator Disk allows PCs to accurately emulate the Minitel terminals. The software is available for IBM PCs and compatibles, Macintosh PCs, BBC/Master/Archimedes and others. The software is simple and easy to use. Logon is automatic and there are extensive facilities for saving and printing screens.

Descriptors — Communications; Viewdata

Operating System — MS DOS; APPLE OPERATING SYSTEM

Special Hardware Requirements — To be used together with a subscription to MINITELnet

Price Range — A

Languages — English

TERM MANAGER

Supplier — Business Simulations Ltd

European Dealers/Distributors — IOTA Consultancy (Netherlands)

General Details — Term Manager is a PC-based structured thesaurus system, for the creation and maintenance of hierarchical thesauri. It is an interactive system, that allows browsing of terms alphabetically or hierarchically, and on-line editing. The full range of term relationships is supported — narrower, broader, related, preferred — and all reciprocal links between terms are automatically maintained whenever changes are made. An optional free-text scope note and user classification code can be added to each term. Term Manager can be used stand-alone to provide a computer-based reference, or run simultaneously with PC-based Cardbox-Plus and Picture Cardbox databases for automatic verification of indexed terms (see Cardbox-Plus and Picture Cardbox), and as the entry point for record retrieval. A thesaurus can be compiled from an ASCII file or database of existing terms. A print facility gives output in a variety of formats, including representation of hierarchical links between terms. A read-only version is available for electronic publishing of thesauri.

Descriptors — Thesaurus control

Operating System — MS DOS

Price Range — A

Languages — English

Reviews — Cardbox-Plus update: pictures and a thesaurus. *Library Micromation News*, 33, September 1991, 2 - 6

TEXPLORE

Supplier — Agate Software Ltd

General Details — Texplore is a simple text retrieval system. It enables the user to search multiple text files for paragraphs containing a word or word-combination. AND, OR, BUT-NOT and abbreviations are allowed. The response is virtually instantaneous irrespective of size of database. This is achieved by pre-indexing the text files, a process which generates highly condensed files relating words to their positions in the text files.

Descriptors — Information retrieval

Operating System — MS DOS

Price Range — A

Languages — English

TEXTMASTER *

Supplier — Bytesmiths Ltd

European Dealers/Distributors — EPMS bv (Netherlands)

General Details — A free-text retrieval package with a full function query language known as LEXIS offering a wide variety of search and viewing options, including graphics handling. Input is from a keyboard or ASCII, Wordstar, or Word Perfect files. Output is possible in a variety of formats via a report generator. The Lexis query language enables simple and powerful searches and searching facilities include use of Boolean logic, nesting, proximity searching, word adjacency, use of search sets, right- and left-hand truncation, index browsing, text string searching etc. A number of different versions of Textmaster are available, each tailored to a different market (eg banking, market research, legal etc.). Textmaster can be run with a worm disk.

Descriptors — Information retrieval; Free text retrieval

Operating System — MS DOS

Price Range — A/B

Languages — English; Dutch; German; Spanish; French

Reviews — Lost, but not forgotten: text-retrieval packages. *PC Magazine*, 2 (5), May 1989.

TEXTO

Supplier — Chemdata S.A.; Chemdata Iberica S.A.; Chemdata Belgium

General Details — TEXTO is a powerful and flexible information management and retrieval system. It has been installed in over 40 different countries and is highly portable, being available for a wide range of operating systems on hardware ranging from mainframe to microcomputer. Applications are simple to set up and easily modified. Fields are variable in length and 10 to 20 indexes (depending on hardware) can be created for each file with the facility to invert multiple fields into each index. Searching includes Boolean operators, right- and left-handed and internal truncation, character masking, range searching etc. Output formats are user-defined and reports can be sorted on one or more fields. Two new versions of TEXTO have recently been released: TEXTO WINDOWS which is available to run under WINDOWS 3.0; TEXTO-GED which incorporates image processing and retrieval into TEXT WINDOWS.

Descriptors — Information retrieval; Image processing

Operating System — MS DOS; UNIX; MS WINDOWS; VMS

Price Range — C

Languages — French; English; German; Spanish; Italian; Portuguese; Russian; Arabic

Reviews — Hall, S., The Sports Council Information Centre's use of Texto. *Library Micromation News*, 29, Sept 1990.

THOT

European Dealers/Distributors — IN2 S.A. (Spain); DOC 6 (Spain); IN2 Computer (Belgium); B33 (France)

General Details — THOT is a French library housekeeping system marketed in Spain under the name THOT (See LIBER). Functions include serials control incorporating subscription and collection management; acquisitions including budget control; cataloguing, retrieval and OPAC — vocabulary control is available during cataloguing; circulation control with optional use of barcodes; customisable screen and print formats and a variety of other general purpose utilities including stock-taking, inter-library loans and parametrisation. The system is multilingual with a wide variety of language versions available.

Descriptors — Integrated library housekeeping system; Serials control; Acquisitions; Cataloguing; OPAC; Inter-library loans

Operating System — MS DOS; PICK; UNIX

Price Range — D

Languages — Spanish; Catalan; English; French; German; Italian; Dutch

TININC

Supplier — IF SrL

General Details — TINinc is an application of the TINman database management system developed by IME (see TINlib). It is used to catalogue engravings, designs and prints.

Descriptors — Information retrieval; Cataloguing

Operating System — MS DOS; UNIX

Languages — Italian

TINLIB

Supplier — IME Ltd

European Dealers/Distributors — Charles University Computing Centre (Czechoslovakia); Mentor Informatik A/S (Denmark); Imexi Oy (Finland); Bull Scicon Services (Greece); Computer & Automation Research Institute (Hungary); IF SrL (Italy); Infopartners (Luxembourg); Bureau IMC (Netherlands); Unilógica (Portugal); DOC 6 (Spain); Unisys España S.A. (Spain); Rola Hard- und Softwareberatung GmbH (Switzerland); Kalhost (Turkey)

General Details — TINlib is a complete system for libraries and information centres, and is designed to meet all of their many and complex requirements, including: Online catalogue, Circulation control, Acquisitions (monographs), Serials control, Data Import, Data Export, Inter-Library loans, Report Generation, CD-ROM interface and Telecommunications. TINlib modules are available separately as well as together in a fully integrated system. The system combines menus with extensive use of function keys to invoke particular tasks, such as inserting a search term, viewing an authority file, inserting data in a new field etc. TINlib uses windows enabling the user to view different areas of the file and to copy data from the windows and amend data within the windows. TINlib's powerful searching facilities include the ability to "Browse and Navigate" through records enabling the searchers to develop ideas as they go along. Also available are various stand-alone products such as an inter-library loans package (TINlend) and a thesaurus management product (TINterm).

Descriptors — Integrated library housekeeping system; Cataloguing; OPAC; Circulation; Acquisitions; Serials control; CD-ROM interface ; Inter-library loans; Communications; Data reformatting

Operating System — MS DOS; UNIX

Price Range — C/D

Languages — English; Spanish; Catalan; Greek; Italian; German; Danish; French; Swedish; Dutch; Hungarian; Czech; Portuguese; Turkish

Reviews — Smith, C., User front-end: IME. *C&L Applications*, 4 (1), July/August 1990.
Tinlib: two applications. *VINE*, 78, May 1990, 4-9.
Crowe, J.A., The use of TINman to automate a library of brewing literature. In: *MS-DOS software for library and information applications*. Edited by Paul Burton. Aldershot, UK: Gower, 1990.
Giaccia, S., FLAN: virtual inter-linking using floppy disks as a local area network. *The Electronic Library*, 7 (3), July 1989.
Leeves, J., *A guide to inter-library loan management systems*. LINC, 1991.

TINPHOTO

Supplier — IF SrL

General Details — TINphoto is an application of the TINman database management system developed by IME (see TINlib). It is used to catalogue photographs.

Descriptors — Information retrieval; Cataloguing

Operating System — MS DOS; UNIX

Languages — Italian

TMS

Supplier — Documedia Systems Ltd

General Details — TMS is stand-alone software for the online creation and maintenance of thesauri. Both an alphabetical and subject display are maintained online and printed if required. Broader, narrower and related terms are supported together with "use for", "use" and "see also" references and scope notes. When a term relationship is entered the reverse relationship is automatically assigned, and the total number of relationships for that term is displayed. The system has multi-lingual capabilities whereby each term may be assigned two alternative terms thus allowing the simultaneous creation of multi-lingual thesauri.

Descriptors — Thesaurus control

Operating System — MS DOS

Price Range — A

Languages — English

TNO ONLINE SEARCH ADMINISTRATOR (TOSA) *

Supplier — CID-TNO

General Details — TOSA runs in conjunction with any communications software supporting a script in background mode (e.g. Mikrotel) to provide administration of online use. TOSA automatically collects certain data, in addition to asking questions of the user, and this information is then used to compile a log book of online use. Sorting and analysis of this information is possible by time, host, database etc. A calculation feature utilises host price lists and current exchange rates to calculate cost per search.

Descriptors — Online monitoring

Operating System — MS DOS

Price Range — A

TOPIC *

Supplier — BIM (Belgium)

General Details — Topic is a full-text search and retrieval system designed for distributed networked computing environments. Topic provides facilities to store, manage, and retrieve any document regardless of its format or location on a network. Employing "Concept Retrieval", Topic features a rule-based approach to searching documents by subject of interest and presenting search results in relevance-ranked order. Topic can be used both for managing internal text and image data, and for external information sources. The Topic Real-Time System automatically monitors live sources of textual information, such as financial newswires or electronic mail, classifies the data and disseminates information according to each individual user's interests. The Topic SQL-Bridge allows Topic full-text databases to be integrated with popular RDBMS products such as ORACLE, Ingres, Informix and Sybase. In addition, Topic provides powerful HyperLink connections to images, annotations and other documents.

Descriptors — Information retrieval; Thesaurus control; Free text retrieval; Image processing

Operating System — MS DOS; UNIX; VMS

Price Range — D

Languages — English

Reviews — Chong, A., Feature Software Review: Topic. *Library Software Review*, 8 (5), September-October 1989.
Doler, K., Verity, rivals have unique relationship. *PC Week*, 6 (44), November 1989.
Freedman, B., Verity upgrades Topic text manager: new version boasts improved query abilities, hypertext features. *PC Week*, 6 (23), June 1989.
Mace, S., Topic upgrade to include Hypertext, query builder, real-time integration. *Info-World*, 11 (26), June 1989.

UNICORN COLLECTION MANAGEMENT SYSTEM

Supplier — Sirsi Ltd

General Details — Unicorn is a fully integrated searching and library housekeeping system running under UNIX and incorporating BRS/Search as its searching facility (see BRS/Search). It is modular in structure and comprises the following: Bibliographic and Inventory Control; Enhanced Public Access; Retrieval Interface Manager; Circulation Control; Academic Reserves; Acquisitions; Serials Control; Authority Control; Electronic Mail; Materials Booking. The system is not menu-driven but uses combinations of keys on the keyboard to invoke functions. Data can be entered at the keyboard or imported in machine-readable form and MARC records are fully supported. The system allows for full text retrieval and any fields can be authority controlled. BRS/Search is used to provide the indexing and searching engine for Unicorn and results in sophisticated online access to the catalogue.

Descriptors — Integrated library housekeeping system; Cataloguing; OPAC; Circulation; Acquisitions; Serials control

Operating System — UNIX

Special Hardware Requirements — Minimum 386- or 486-based PCs

Price Range — E

Languages — English

Reviews — Haines, M., The year of the Unicorn: a review of the first year's experience with the Unicorn Collection Management System at the King's Fund Centre. *Program*, 26 (2), April 1992.
SIRSI's Unicorn at the King's Fund. *VINE*, 84, October 1991.
SIRSI's Unicorn. *VINE*, 81, December 1990.

V-K UITLEENSYSTEEM *

Supplier — P.M. van Velsen / A. Knevel

General Details — A library loans system.

Descriptors — Circulation

Operating System — MS DOS

VICOM *

Supplier — Vicom Ltd

General Details — VICOM is a fully integrated software package that offers both ASCII and viewdata communications. It also provides full VT100 emulation. Any baud rate between 50 and 19200 can be supported, as well as the more usual 300/300, 1200/1200 and 1200/75. An auto log-on facility is included, in which time delays can be added where ASCII databases have multi-level log-on. VICOM allows simultaneous activities to be performed, e.g. at the same time as sending a file, a previously received document can be printed while a new message is being created. Clear on-screen commands are shown, which can be selected by using a mouse; additional function keys are available at the click of a mouse to send often-repeated commands. File transfer using Xmodem and binary protocols ensures error-free transmission. Multiple windows can be used to perform several tasks simultaneously. Pages of viewdata can be saved, and page numbers noted for automatic recall. Pages can also be "cut and pasted" into an ASCII document.

Descriptors — Communications; Viewdata; Downloading

Operating System — MS DOS; APPLE OPERATING SYSTEM

Price Range — A

Languages — English

Reviews — VICOM communications software for all levels? *Communications 2000*, 10, November 1990.
Dennis, T., Best comms software. *Which Computer*, March 1989.

VISYS

Supplier — K.A. Spencer

General Details — VISYS is a Video-tape Cataloguing System suitable for educational institutions, commercial video programme libraries, media researchers, and anyone else concerned with handling information and archives in the film and video-tape media. VISYS permits the creation of, and search and retrieval from, a database of information on each video-tape or film. In addition, VISYS features an option to generate a full cross-reference printed catalogue of all material in the database. The VISYS data set includes title, note, source, month and year, up to eight keywords, and up to three people (i.e. Director/Producer/Actor etc). Programme titles can be entered, amended, deleted, and searched by source, people and keywords. Full printed output is available, including a full catalogue, cross referenced by source, people, and keywords. Other features include: unique password for data protection, up to 10,000 titles (hard disk), and 10,000 people per index; keyword dictionary of 990 words; titles and notes of up to 158 characters each; and an online manual. (See also JISYS)

Descriptors — Information retrieval; Personal bibliographic database; Reference management; Media control

Operating System — MS DOS; RISC OS (Archimedes)

Price Range — A

Languages — English

VRIND *

Supplier — D.R.F. van Bremen Informatica Advies bv

General Details — No details supplied for this software.

VTEXT

Supplier — Text and Video Systems Ltd

General Details — VTEXT is a free text search system with a command language which has been designed for ease of use. VTEXT can be used for storing and retrieving all kinds of textual information, including reports, correspondence, electronic mail, patents, marketing and company information, newspaper cuttings etc. It can also be used in combination with interactive video for the retrieval of both text and pictures.

Descriptors — Information retrieval; Media control

Operating System — MS DOS; VMS

Price Range — C

Languages — English

VUBIS

Supplier — ODIS

European Dealers/Distributors — ODIS Pays-Bas; ODIS France

General Details — VUBIS is a fully integrated library housekeeping system with powerful search tools. Staff from the libraries of VUB and Eindhoven Technical University were involved in developing the system. Online communication with other library systems such as PICA and DOBIS/LIBIS is possible. The system is used by small libraries with several thousand volumes up to large institutions with over 3 million loans and 100,000 acquisitions per year. It is a multi-user system; under DOS it can support up to 30 users, depending on the power of the processor. All updating is carried out in real time. VUBIS consists of five principal parts covering the functions of cataloguing, lending, serials administration, acquisitions and OPAC.

Descriptors — Integrated library housekeeping system; Acquisitions; Cataloguing; Circulation; OPAC; Serials control

Operating System — MS DOS; UNIX; VMS

Languages — French; Dutch; English; German; Spanish

Reviews — Baker, J., Serials control at the Technische Universiteit Eindhoven. *VINE*, 87, June 1992.

WINFORM

Supplier — Jan de Winter Adviesbureau

General Details — Winform is a cataloguing and loans system providing searching on standard fields such as author, title and one or more keywords. Free text up to a maximum of 2 A4 pages can be entered.

Descriptors — Cataloguing; Circulation

Operating System — MS DOS

Price Range — A

Languages — Dutch; English

WORDCRUNCHER *

Supplier — Electronic Text Corporation (US)

European Dealers/Distributors — International Brainware (Netherlands)

General Details — Wordcruncher is an indexing system. DOS text files are indexed using WC INDEX and manipulated using WC VIEW. It is well suited to a variety of languages and a thesaurus can also be created. Search facilities are sophisticated. Output includes Book-style and KWIC indexes.

Descriptors — Indexing

Operating System — MS DOS; MS WINDOWS; OS/2

Price Range — A

Languages — English

XMODEM PC *

Supplier — BVR Vedder

General Details — A telecommunications package which can operate between 110 and 9600 baud. Files may be up or downloaded using either Xon/Xoff protocol or the Xmodem protocol of Ward Christensen. The built-in editor works with Wordstar commands and allows two files to be edited at the same time using a window technique. Up to 40 commands or strings, each of up to 72 characters may be stored under function keys to enable easy storage and transmission of passwords and search terms. Comments are issued in German.

Descriptors — Communications; Online search aid; Downloading

Operating System — MS DOS

Price Range — A

Languages — German

ZYINDEX

Supplier — Zylab Corporation (US)

European Dealers/Distributors — MSC Information Retrieval Technologies (Netherlands); Softkey (Netherlands)

General Details — ZYINDEX's main application is to find information out of large numbers of separate files such as those from word processors and letters. This means that it requires no real records with their special structure of separate fields, but works with complete files. Within files it offers full-text search capabilities, with AND, OR and AND NOT operators. Files from a wide variety of word processing programs can be read and indexed directly and ZyIndex works with files in their native format and does not interfere with directory locations. The software creates a thesaurus and indexes can be viewed.

Descriptors — Information retrieval; File indexing

Operating System — MS DOS; MS WINDOWS; UNIX

Price Range — A

Languages — English; Dutch; French

Reviews — Côté, R and Diehl, S., Searching for common threads. *BYTE*, June 1992.
Marshall, P., Textbase champ gets GUI goodies but keeps speed. *Info World*, 13 (31), August 5, 1991.
Marshall, P. et al., Combing the Stacks. *Info World*, 12 (52), December 24/31, 1990.

Supplier Index

Supplier Index

AB FORETAGSSIMULERING

Address Trotningatan
411 14 Göteborg
Sweden

Telephone +46 31 17 92 70

Software Mikro Polydoc

ABACUS RESEARCH AG

Address Rorschacherstrasse 170
PO Box 694
CH-9006 St Gallen
Switzerland

Telephone +41 71 259 325
Fax +41 71 253 860

Software DataFlex

ABACUS SOFTWARE LTD

Address 13 Pall Mall
London SW1Y 5LU
UK

Telephone +44 71 930 4884
Telex 931756 WPSGRP G
Fax +44 71 839 7445

Software STAR

ACCRET

Address Glashuset
134 00 Gustausberg
Sweden

Telephone +46 766 35530

Software Knosys; Clarity

ADDA, SCP (INFORMÀTICA SARRIÀ)

Address c/o Negrevernis, 24 - 28
Botiga
08034 Barcelona
Spain

Telephone +34 3 204 7005
Fax +34 3 204 7203

Software Micro-VTLS

ADLIB INFORMATION SYSTEMS LTD

Address Marlborough Business Centre
Claverton House
Pelhams Court
London Road
Marlborough
Wiltshire SN8 2AB
UK

Telephone +44 672 515525
Fax +44 672 515828

Software ADLIB Lite

THE ADVISORY UNIT FOR MICROTECHNOLOGY IN EDUCATION

Address Wheathampstead Education Centre
Butterfield Road
Wheathampstead
AL4 8PY
UK

Telephone +44 582 830273

Software ORIEL; QUEST

AGATE SOFTWARE LTD

Address Agate House
Wilton Drive
Whitley Bay
Tyne & Wear NE25 9PU
UK

Telephone +44 91 252 0488

Software Texplore

AGENCE FRANÇAISE INFORMATIQUE

Address Rue de la Maison-Rouge
77322 Lognes
Marne-la-Vallée
France

Telephone +33 1 60 17 12 34

Software Afibyblos

AIDEL

Address Rue de la Poste
Le Cheylas-Bourg
38570 Goncelin
France

Telephone +33 76 71 84 09
Fax +33 76 71 81 92

Software SUPERDOC

ALDODA INTERNATIONAL LTD

Address 27 Elizabeth Mews
London
NW3 4UH
UK

Telephone +44 71 586 5686
Telex 94018064 ALDA G
Fax +44 71 586 9625

Software Infodial

AMTEK COMPUTER SERVICES LTD

Address Intersection House
110-120 Birmingham Road
West Bromwich
West Midlands B70 6RX
UK

Telephone +44 21 525 8903
Telex 338 449
Fax +44 21 553 3956

Software LIBMAN

ANDOR INFORMATION BROKERS

Address Jan Campertlaan 14
2741 AB Waddinxveen
Netherlands

Telephone +31 1828 17778

Software DIVA

ANTHESIS

Address 1854 Rue des Sources
14204 Hérouville Saint Clair Cedex
France

Telephone +33 31 44 02 01
Fax +33 31 94 63 05

Software Babylone Documentation

APPLE COMPUTER UK LTD

Address 6 Roundwood Avenue
Stockley Park
Uxbridge
Middlesex UB11 1BB
UK

Telephone +44 81 569 1199

Software MacTerminal 2.3

APRIL COMPUTING EXECUTIVE LTD

Address Chestnut Farm
Tarvin Road
Frodsham
Cheshire WA6 6XN
UK

Telephone +44 928 35868
Telex 946240 CWEASY G
Fax +44 928 35352

Software LITREF

ASSOCIATED KNOWLEDGE SYSTEMS

Address Amen House
Bedale
N. Yorkshire DL8 1XA
UK

Telephone +44 677 425101
Fax +44 677 423568

Software Assassin PC

ATBIB BV

Address Hollandsestraat 2
B-2300 Turnhout
Belgium

Telephone +32 14 41 77 75

Software ATBiB

AUDIO-VISUAL ORGANISATION

Address 21 Lambeth Court
Putney Bridge Road
Wandsworth
London SW18 1HN
UK

Telephone +44 81 871 2979

Software Livelink

AUTOMATIACION DE BIBLIOTECAS

Address Hileras, 8
4th floor, Appartment D
28013 Madrid
Spain

Software SABINI

B.H. BLACKWELL LTD (LIBRARY BOOKSELLING DIVISION)

Address Hythe Bridge Street
Oxford OX1 2ET
UK

Telephone +44 865 792792
Telex 851-83118
Fax +44 865 791438

Software PC-Order/PC-Order Plus/PC Query

B.H. BLACKWELL LTD (PERIODICALS DIVISION)

Address Hythe Bridge Street
Oxford OX1 2ET
UK

Telephone +44 865 792792 x329
Telex 851-83118
Fax +44 865 791438

Software ISIS; Blackwell's Connect

B33

Address 85-86 Avenue Thiers
33100 Bordeaux
France

Telephone +33 56 32 28 56

Software THOT

BARCELONA TECNOLOGIA, S.A.

Address Balmes, 163 pral., 1
08008 Barcelona
Spain

Telephone +34 3 415 9517
Fax +34 3 415 5236

Software MDUP

BHS

Address 17 Rue Théodore-Maillart
76600 Le Havre
France

Telephone +33 35 43 47 89
Fax +33 35 42 64 28

Software Bifac

BIBLIOTECA NACIONAL, DIVISAO DE INFORMATICA

Address Campo Grande 83
1751 Lisbon
Portugal

Telephone +351 1 7978822
Fax +351 1 7933607

Software Micro CDS/ISIS

BIBLIOTHEKS CENTRUM SVERIGE AB (BIC)

Address Box 113
351 04 Växjö
Sweden

Telephone +46 470 40045
Fax +46 470 45078

Software HEADFAST;
HEADFAST/CD;
HEADFORM;
HEADLINE;
HEADSET;
BiblioMac; MikroMARC

BILANEY CONSULTANTS GMBH

Address Schirmerstrasse 23
4000 Düsseldorf 1
Germany

Telephone +49 211 36 40 43
Fax +49 211 164 91 77

Software Reference Manager

BILANEY CONSULTANTS LTD

Address	St Julians Sevenoaks Kent TN15 0RX UK
Telephone	+44 732 450002
Fax	+44 732 450003
Software	Reference Manager

BIM

Address	Kwikstraat 4 B-3078 Everberg Belgium
Telephone	+32 2 759 59 25
Fax	+32 2 759 47 95
Software	Topic

BIOSOFT

Address	49 Bateman Street Cambridge CB2 1LR UK
Telephone	+44 223 68622
Fax	+44 223 312873
Software	AutoBiblio; Refsys Super

BLACKWELLS SCIENTIFIC PUBLICATIONS

Address	Osney Mead Oxford OX2 0EL UK
Telephone	+44 865 240201
Software	ideaList

BNF-FULMER

Address	Wantage Business Park Wantage Oxfordshire OX12 9BJ UK
Telephone	+44 235 772992
Telex	837166
Fax	+44 235 771144
Software	STRIDE

BONNTEXT

Address	Clemens August Strasse, 2-4 5300 Bonn 1 Germany
Telephone	+49 228 630222
Software	Knosys; Clarity

BORGEAUD-INFORMATIQUE

Address	BP 350 92541 Montrouge Cedex France
Telephone	+33 1 47 35 54 40
Telex	632 740
Software	Biblix

THE BRITISH LIBRARY NATIONAL BIBLIOGRAPHIC SERVICE

Address Boston Spa
Wetherby
West Yorkshire
LS23 7BQ
UK

Telephone +44 937 546585
Telex 557831
Fax +44 937 546568

Software BLAISE Recorder; Grateful Med

BRS SOFTWARE PRODUCTS BENELUX

Address Gele Rijdersplein 16
6811 AP Arnhem
Netherlands

Telephone +31 85 579600
Fax +31 85 438636

Software BRS/Search

BRS SOFTWARE PRODUCTS EUROPE

Address 11 Weymouth Street
London
W1N 3FG
UK

Telephone +44 71 580 5271
Fax +44 71 436 0997

Software BRS/Search

BRS SOFTWARE PRODUCTS SCANDINAVIA A/S

Address Bredgade 36
DK-1260 Copenhagen K.
Denmark

Telephone +45 33 14 35 00
Fax +45 33 14 40 66

Software BRS/Search

BULL SCICON SERVICES

Address 3 Skra Str & Syngrou Ave
176 73 Kallithera
Athens
Greece

Telephone +30 1 9525 255/256
Fax +30 1 9588 632

Software TINlib

BUREAU IMC

Address Mathenesserlaan 294
3021 HV Rotterdam
Netherlands

Telephone +31 10 478 02 04
Fax +31 10 478 08 72

Software TINlib

BUSINESS COMPUTERS HILSBOROUGH LTD

Address 141 Dromore Road
Hilsborough
Co. Down BT26 6JA
N. Ireland
UK

Telephone +44 846 683791
Fax +44 846 683798

Software Heritage

BUSINESS FILE LTD

Address Inst. of Research & Dev.
Birmingham Research Park
Vincent Drive
Birmingham B15 2SQ
UK

Telephone +44 21 414 1814
Fax +44 21 414 1861

Software STRIX

BUSINESS SIMULATIONS LTD

Address 30 St James's Street
London
SW1A 1HB
UK

Telephone +44 71 925 0636
Telex 95513 SCRIVS G
Fax +44 71 925 0638

Software Cardbox-Plus; Picture Cardbox; Term Manager

BVR VEDDER

Address Weissenburgerstrasse 16
8546 Thalmessing
Germany

Telephone +49 9173 1216

Software XMODEM PC

BYTESMITHS LTD

Address 12 Redden Court Road
Harold Wood
Essex RM3 0XA
UK

Telephone +44 708 345150

Software Textmaster

CAIRS INFORMATION SYSTEMS

Address Leatherhead Food Research Association
Randalls Road
Leatherhead
Surrey KT22 7RY
UK

Telephone +44 372 376761
Telex 929846
Fax +44 372 386228

Software CAIRS IMS; CAIRS LMS

CALLHAVEN PLC

Address 74 Rivington Street
London
EC2A 3AY
UK

Telephone +44 71 410 9191
Fax +44 71 410 9195

Software MARS; FreeForm

CAMBRIDGE SOFTWARE

Address PO Box 3
Ely
Cambridge CB7 4AX
UK

Telephone +44 353 664444/+44 860 410121

Software RASMUS

CART SYSTEMS

Address PO Box 11148
3004 EC Rotterdam
Netherlands

Telephone +31 10 437 6628

Software Biblio-Plus

CAT BENELUX

Address Dorpsweg 78
1697 KD Schellinkhont
Netherlands

Telephone +31 2293 1682

Software Freebase

CD-BASE LTD

Address Assets House
Elverton Street
London SW1P 2QG
UK

Telephone +44 71 828 2355
Fax +44 71 821 5684

Software Full/Text

CEFIS

Address Facultés universitaires Notre Dame de la Paix
Rue de Bruxelles 61
B-5000 Namur
Belgium

Telephone +32 81 72 50 60
Telex 59222 FAC NAM B
Fax +32 81 72 50 64

Software GIBUS

CELTIP COMPUTERS

Address AppleCentre
Lower Mill Street
Kidderminster
Worcestershire DY10 2JG
UK

Telephone +44 562 822222
Fax +44 562 67202

Software Mac School Library

CHARLES UNIVERSITY COMPUTING CENTRE

Address Ovocny trh 5
116 36 Praha 1
Czechoslovakia

Telephone +42 2 260 641 x306
Fax +42 2 264 223

Software TINlib

CHEM RESEARCH GMBH

Address Beethovenstrasse 7b
6000 Frankfurt 1
Germany

Telephone +49 69 7411114
Fax +49 69 740496

Software EndNote

CHEMDATA BELGIUM

Address Rue Dautzenberg, 38
B-1050 Bruxelles
Belgium

Telephone +32 2 648 27 70
Fax +32 2 648 36 93

Software TEXTO; LOGOTEX; DV-ONE; PATCHWORK

CHEMDATA IBERICA S.A.

Address Alcala, 101-2.pl.
28009 Madrid
Spain

Telephone +34 1 435 2202/435 2263
Telex 232621 - 1174
Fax +34 1 431 4556

Software TEXTO; LOGOTEX; DV-ONE; PATCHWORK

CHEMDATA S.A.

Address 17 Quai Gillet
69316 Lyon Cedex 04
France

Telephone +33 78 29 70 55
Telex 306 137

Software TEXTO; LOGOTEX; DV-ONE; PATCHWORK

CHERWELL SCIENTIFIC PUBLISHING

Address The Magdalen Centre
Oxford Science Park
Oxford
OX4 4GA
UK

Telephone +44 865 784800
Fax +44 865 784801

Software EndNote

CID-TNO

Address PO Box 36
2600 AA Delft
Netherlands

Telephone +31 15 560825
Telex 38071 ZPTNO NL
Fax +31 15 560825

Software TNO Online Search Administrator (TOSA)

CIPAL

Address Technische Schoolstraat 43A
B-2440 Geel
Belgium

Telephone +32 14 57 62 11
Telex 73 482 (CIPAL B)
Fax +32 14 58 35 00

Software CIBIS (Cipal Bibliotheek Systeem)

COBIDOC BV

Address PO Box 16601
1001 RC Amsterdam
Netherlands

Telephone +31 20 6223955
Telex 18766
Fax +31 20 6222556

Software Mikrotel; STN Express

COI-VLABRIC

Address Interleuvenlaan 16
B-3001 Leuven
Belgium

Software DOBILUS

COMMUNICATOR SOFTWARE ENGINEERING BV

Address Staringlaan 21-28
2741 GC Waddinxveen
Netherlands

Telephone +31 1828 10444

Software Supercom

COMPAGNIE D'APPLICATION ET D'ASSISTANCE EN DOCUMENTATION (CAPADOC)

Address 62 Rue de Paris
92100 Boulogne
France

Telephone +33 1 46 03 10 85
Fax +33 1 46 03 98 90

Software STN Express

COMPUTER & AUTOMATION RESEARCH INSTITUTE

Address Hungarian Academy of Sciences
MTA - SZTAKI
1111 Budapest
Hungary

Telephone +36 1 1611 257
Fax +36 1 1667 503

Software TINlib

COMPUTERS UNLIMITED

Address 2 The Business Centre
Colindeep Lane
London NW9 6DU
UK

Telephone +44 81 200 8282

Software MicroPhone II

COMSYS

Address 49 Sygrou Ave & M Botsari
11742 Athens
Greece

Telephone +30 1 9223 283

Software Analogio

COMWARE INTERNATIONAL LTD

Address Unit 25, Boundary Business Centre
Boundary Road
Woking
Surrey GU21 5BH
UK

Telephone +44 483 761686
Fax +44 483 730387

Software Relay Gold

CORALPLAN LTD

Address 27 Elizabeth Mews
London
NW3 4UH
UK

Telephone +44 71 483 0119
Fax +44 71 483 0120

Software Teletel Emulator Disk

CRDP

Address 6 Rue Sainte-Catherine
86034 Poitiers
France

Telephone +33 49 88 11 70

Software Memolog 2

CRISTAD

Address Zac de Mercieres
60200 Compiegne
France

Software Basil

D.A.F.A. DATA AB

Address Section 220
PO Box 34101
100 26 Stockholm
Sweden

Telephone +46 8 67 92 80
Telex 10366 FOAS

Software Micro CDS/ISIS

D.B.A. ASSOCIAZIONE PER LA DOCUMENTAZIONE LE BIBLIOTECHE E GLI ARCHIVI

Address Largo F.lli Alinari 11
50123 Florence
Italy

Telephone +39 55 283596
Fax +39 55 218620

Software Micro CDS/ISIS

D.I.C.E. LTD

Address 46 Anagnostopoulou St
10673 Athens
Greece

Telephone +30 1 360 6450

Software LIBRI

D.R.F. VAN BREMEN INFORMATICA ADVIES BV

Address Stadhouderslaan 12
2517 HW Den Haag
Netherlands

Telephone +31 70 3624777

Software Vrind; Strix; dLib

D & R SOFTWARE SERVICES

Address PO Box 30052
6803 AB Arnhem
Netherlands

Telephone +31 85 256060

Software PC Stairs

DABIS

Address Heiligenstadterstrasse 215
1190 Vienna
Austria

Telephone +43 222 372505

Software BIS-LOK

DABIS-GESELLSCHAFT FÜR DATENBANK-INFORMATIONS-SYSTEME MBH

Address Palmaille 106
2000 Hamburg 50
Germany

Telephone +49 40 381764/65
Fax +49 40 3800563

Software BIS-LOK

DANTEK

Address Vestergade 41
DK-8600 Silkeborg
Denmark

Software BIBLIOMATIK

DARK STAR INFORMATION SYSTEMS

Address 12 St Peter's Court
Middleborough
Colchester
Essex CO1 1WD
UK

Telephone +44 206 578224
Fax +44 206 578504

Software STAR

DATA ACCESS EUROPE AB

Address Gathes Vag 147
439 00 Onsala
Sweden

Telephone +46 30 063 626
Fax +46 30 060 442

Software DataFlex

DATA ACCESS EUROPE DEUTSCHLAND GMBH

Address Bahnstrasse 15
6382 Friedrichsdorf
Germany

Telephone +49 61 727 5014
Fax +49 61 727 2079

Software DataFlex

DATA KONCEPT

Address Copenhagen
Denmark

Telephone +45 39 66 10 22
Fax +45 39 66 12 22

Software Aleph/PC

DATA TREK INTERNATIONAL

Address 28 Rue Basfroi
75011 Paris
France

Telephone +33 1 43 70 88 17
Fax +33 1 43 70 67 23

Software Data Trek

DATA TREK UK

Address Dugard House
Peartree Road
Colchester
Essex CO3 5JX
UK

Telephone +44 206 369233
Fax +44 206 369632

Software Data Trek

DATABASIX INFORMATION SYSTEMS BV

Address PO Box 179
3454 ZK De Meern
Netherlands

Telephone +31 3406 62455
Fax +31 3406 65033

Software ADLIB Lite

DATACENTRALEN

Address Retortvej 8
DK-2500 Valby
Denmark

Software PC Info

DATAFLEX SERVICES LTD

Address DataNet House
114-116 Curtain Road
London EC2A 3AH
UK

Telephone +44 71 729 4460
Fax +44 71 739 1247

Software DataFlex

DATASOFT LTD

Address 7-8 Ditton Street
Ilminster
Somerset
TA19 0BQ
UK

Telephone +44 460 57001
Fax +44 460 57060

Software Datatalk

DATAWARE

Address 23 Rue Laugier
75017 Paris
France

Telephone +33 1 47 66 00 36
Fax +33 1 46 22 13 62

Software Influx

DAUSTRAUB SOFTWARE GMBH

Address Fritschgasse 1
5020 Salzburg
Austria

Telephone +43 662 658 2237
Fax +43 662 658 28

Software DataFlex

DAWSON TECHNOLOGY LTD

Address Cannon House
Park Farm Road
Folkestone
Kent CT19 5EE
UK

Telephone +44 303 850537
Telex 96392
Fax +44 303 850440

Software OASIS; OASIS-AIM; OASIS-SMS

DC INFORMATIK LTD

Address Danmarksvej 30 M2
DK-8660 Skanderborg
Denmark

Telephone +45 86 52 48 44

Fax +45 86 51 18 80

Software DCTS Periodicals Control System

DECALOG

Address 1 Rue Georges Bizet
26000 Valence
France

Telephone +33 75 55 22 04

Software Paprika

DECISION TECHNOLOGY

Address 7 St Johns Road
East Molesey
Surrey
KT8 9JH
UK

Telephone +44 81 979 5533
Fax +44 81 979 7045

Software Labelmaker

DEINFOR S.A.

Address Ausias Marc 26 pl. 7
08010 Barcelona
Spain

Telephone +34 3 301 82 35
Fax +34 3 317 62 24

Software Aleph/PC

DIALOG INFORMATION SERVICES

Address PO Box 188
Oxford
OX1 5AX
UK

Telephone +44 865 326226
Telex 837704
Fax +44 865 736354

Software DIALOGLINK

DOC 6

Address Tuset 21 6, 3
08006 Barcelona
Spain

Telephone +34 3 414 0679
Fax +34 3 201 6357

Software Data Trek; TINlib; SABINI; INMAGIC Plus; SearchMAGIC; CLASS; THOT; SOD; Reference Manager

DOCUMEDIA SYSTEMS LTD

Address 11 Colthrop Way
Thatcham
Newbury
Berkshire RG13 4LW
UK

Telephone +44 635 876800
Fax +44 635 876480

Software CALM; CLASS; TMS; OpAcc; Picture Frame; Syllabus

DOLPHIN COMPUTER SERVICES LTD

Address	5 Mercian Close Watermoor End Cirencester Gloucestershire GL7 1LT UK
Telephone	+44 285 650906/659291
Fax	+44 285 656941
Software	Lexicon

DYNIX FRANCE

Address	30 Avenue de l'Europe 78140 Vélizy- Villacoublay France
Telephone	+33 1 30 67 21 00
Fax	+33 1 30 70 68 69
Software	Dynix

DYNIX LIBRARY SYSTEMS (IRELAND) LTD

Address	75 Haddington Road Ballsbridge Dublin 4 Ireland
Telephone	+353 1 681 366
Fax	+353 1 683 230
Software	Dynix

DYNIX LIBRARY SYSTEMS (UK) LTD

Address	Quay South Salamander Quay Park Lane Harefield, Uxbridge Middlesex UB9 6NY UK
Telephone	+44 895 824091
Fax	+44 895 822968
Software	Dynix

EDINBURGH UNIVERSITY LIBRARY

Address	George Square Edinburgh EH8 9LJ UK
Telephone	+44 31 667 1011
Fax	+44 31 667 9780
Software	SALBIN PC

ELEA LTD

Address	50-52 Valtetsiou Street 10681 Athens Greece
Telephone	+30 1 360 2335/5535
Fax	+30 1 360 6770
Software	LIBRARY 2000

ENTITY Software

Address Lindestraat 12
3297 XM Puttershoek
Netherlands

Telephone +31 1856 2523
Fax +31 1042 67818

Software ModiFile, the convenient converter

EPMS BV

Address Terhorst 19
6262 NA Banholt
Netherlands

Telephone +31 4457 2275
Fax +31 4457 2148

Software MagicKey; BiB/SEARCH; Textmaster; HEADFAST; HEADFAST/CD; HEADFORM; HEADLINE; HEADSET; ELROND; INMAGIC Plus; SearchMAGIC; MULTI Adaptor; MARC Adaptor; KAWare; Blueberry; Data Magician; RefWriter; BiB/TRANS; FILTER

ESRIN

Address Online Services
Via Galileo Galilei
00044 Frascati
Rome
Italy

Telephone +39 6941801

Software Mikrotel

EUROPÉRIODIQUES - SWETS FRANCE

Address BP104 - Parc d'Activités de Pissaloup
78191 Trappes Cedex
France

Software SAILS

EUROSCIENCE

Address PO Box 408
3720 AK Bilthoven
Netherlands

Telephone +31 30 293906
Fax +31 30 285772

Software ModiFile, the convenient converter

EUROSOFT AB

Address PO Box 10331
434 01 Kungsbacka
Sweden

Telephone +46 300 19530
Fax +46 300 70910

Software DataFlex

EUROSOFT NORGE A/S

Address Dronningen 0287
Oslo 2
Norway

Telephone +47 2 559 966
Fax +47 2 438 769

Software DataFlex

EUROTEC CONSULTANTS LTD

Address Aldham House
Hadleigh
Ipswich
Suffolk IP7 6BQ
UK

Telephone +44 473 824470
Fax +44 473 824408

Software LIBRARIAN

EUROTELEMATICA

Address Placa Berenguer, 1
08002 Barcelona
Spain

Telephone +34 3 310 7408/310 7766
Fax +34 3 319 2823

Software ABSYS

EX LIBRIS S.A.

Address 38 Boulevard Napolèon 1er.
BP 1163
L-2210
Luxembourg

Telephone +352 446 556
Fax +352 453 076

Software Aleph/PC

FAXON EUROPE BV

Address Hogehilweg 10
1101 CC Amsterdam
Netherlands

Software MicroLinx

FAXON UK LTD

Address Dormer House
15 Dormer Place
Leamington Spa
CV32 5AA
UK

Telephone +44 926 450424
Fax +44 926 450616

Software MicroLinx

FIZ TECHNIK E.V.

Address Ostbahnhofstrasse 13
PO Box 60 05 47
6000 Frankfurt/M 1
Germany

Telephone +49 69 43 08 0
Telex 4 189 459 fizt d

Software Sherlock

FLOYD RATCLIFFE CONSULTANCY SERVICES LTD

Address 2 The Crescent
Leatherhead
Surrey
KT22 8EE
UK

Telephone +44 372 376423
Fax +44 372 386577

Software LICON

FORMAT PRODUCTS FOR COMPUTERS LTD

Address Goods Wharf
Goods Road
Belper
Derbyshire DE5 1UU
UK

Telephone +44 773 820011
Telex 377532
Fax +44 773 820206

Software Knowledgebase

FORREZ

Address Ijzerenmolenstraat 74
B-3001 Heverlee
Belgium

Software BIDOC

FRASER WILLIAMS (SCIENTIFIC SYSTEMS) LTD

Address London House
London Road South
Poynton
Cheshire SK12 1YP
UK

Telephone +44 625 876711

Software DARC-CHEMLINK

FT PROFILE

Address PO Box 12
Sunbury-on-Thames
Middlesex
TW16 7UO
UK

Telephone +44 932 761 444
Fax +44 932 761 425

Software FT Profile Freeway

GENESYS SOFTWARE-VERTRIEBS GMBH

Address PO Box 19
8062 Markt Indersdorf
Germany

Telephone +49 8136 7061
Fax +49 8136 6164

Software Genesys SIE9751; I&D Software; Synopsys

GERMAN COMMISSION FOR UNESCO

Address Colmanstrasse 15
5300 Bonn 1
Germany

Telephone +49 228 692096
Fax +49 228 636912

Software Micro CDS/ISIS

GESTION BUSINESS CONCEPT

Address Tour Eiffel
2 Rue de Bourets
92150 Suresnes
France

Telephone +33 1 47 28 61 33
Fax +33 1 47 28 61 34

Software Alexandrie II

GLOMAS DEUTSCHLAND GMBH

Address Lansbergerstrasse 199
8000 Munich 21
Germany

Telephone +49 89 57 1037
Fax +49 89 570 5127

Software STAR

HARWELL COMPUTER POWER LTD

Address Curie Avenue
Harwell
Oxford
OX11 0QW
UK

Telephone +44 235 834606
Telex 83525
Fax +44 235 835186

Software Status/PC; CORA

HAYES MICROCOMPUTER PRODUCTS, INC

Address 1 Roundwood Avenue
Stockley Park
Uxbridge
Middlesex
UB11 1AE
UK

Telephone +44 81 841 1858

Software Smartcom II;
Smartcom III

HEAD SOFTWARE INTERNATIONAL

Address Oxted Mill
Spring Lane
Oxted
Surrey RH8 9PB
UK

Telephone +44 883 717057
Fax +44 883 712327

Software HEADFAST;
HEADFAST/CD;
ELROND; HEADFORM;
HEADLINE; HEADSET

HENELL OY

Address Kiukainen
Finland

Software OORNINKI

HILBERINK COMPUTERTECHNIEK

Address Boven Vredenburg 65 (HC)
3511 CW Utrecht
Netherlands

Telephone +31 30 314744

Software Bido

IBR

Address Budapest
Hungary

Telephone +36 1 156 5062

Software Aleph/PC

ICL DATA A/S

Address Lautrupbjerg 1
DK-2750 Ballerup
Denmark

Software RC-LIB

IDC-KTHB

Address Valhallavagen 81
100 44 Stockholm
Sweden

Telephone +46 8 7908955
Telex 10389 kthb s
Fax +46 8 109199

Software STN Express

IDE

Address Kamerlingh Onnesdreef 7
3146 BG Maasluis
Netherlands

Telephone +31 1899 23711

Software CAIRS-LMS;
CAIRS-IMS

IF SRL

Address Viale Don Minzoni 39
50129 Firenze
Italy

Telephone +39 55 500 1357/8
Fax +39 55 500 1363

Software TINinc; TINphoto;
TINlib

IMAGO LOGICA

Address Cort van der Lindenstraat
4-A
2288 EV Rijswijk
Netherlands

Telephone +31 70 3901061
Fax +31 70 3995171

Software Artemis; Image Finder;
Superfile; Colossus

IME LTD

Address 140-142 St John Street
London
EC1V 4JT
UK

Telephone +44 71 253 1177
Fax +44 71 608 3599

Software TINlib

IMEXI OY

Address Kyläsepantio 1
04250 Kerava
Finland

Telephone +358 0 248 022
Fax +358 0 294 4288

Software TINlib

IN2 COMPUTER

Address Chaussée de la Hulpe 177
B-1170 Bruxelles
Belgium

Telephone +32 2 720 92 58

Software THOT

IN2 S.A.

Address Avda. Diagonal 652-656
Edificio B, 80-2a
08034 Barcelona
Spain

Telephone +34 3 280 43 34
Fax +34 3 280 40 64

Software THOT

INFO 3 D

Address 53 Rue Albert-Samain
BP 244
56335 Villeneuve-d'Ascq Cedex
France

Telephone +33 20 91 25 10

Software Logabib

INFOKRAFT LTD

Address 104 Athinin Ave
10442 Athens
Greece

Telephone +30 1 514 3088/9

Software Infokraft Library System

INFOPARTNERS S.A.

Address Airport Center
2e Étage
5 Rue Höhenhof
1736 Senningberg
Luxembourg

Telephone +352 34981 456

Software TINlib

INFORMATION AUTOMATION LTD

Address Penbryn
Bronant
Aberystwyth
Dyfed SY23 4TJ
UK

Telephone +44 97 421 302
Fax +44 97 421 682

Software FILTER; Online Search Tutor Junior (OST Junior); GRIPS-Learn; q-CAL BiB/Search; ACOM; RefWriter

INFORMATION SYSTEMS DESIGN

Address 31 Penarth Grove
Binley
Coventry CV3 2PH
UK

Telephone +44 203 650285

Software LibraryPac 1; LibraryPac2/Library Pac 3

INFORMATION UND KOMMUNIKATION

Address Hartmann von Aue Strasse 9
7801 Freiburg-Au
Germany

Telephone +49 761 407543

Software PC Master; Infodown; Infolog; Infobank; Infotrans

INFORMED BUSINESS SERVICES

Address 25 Old Street
London EC1V 9HL
UK

Telephone +44 71 490 2811
Fax +44 71 490 4068

Software Amitel

INSOFT LTD

Address 179-181 Whiteladies Road
Clifton
Bristol BS8 2RY
UK

Telephone +44 272 239179
Fax +44 272 239457

Software Recall Plus

INSTITUTE OF DEVELOPMENT STUDIES

Address University of Sussex
Brighton BN1 9RE
UK

Telephone +44 273 606261
Telex 877997IDSBTNG
Fax +44 273 621202

Software Micro CDS/ISIS

INSTITUTO DE INFORMACION Y DOCUMENTACION EN CIENCIA Y TECNOLOGIA

Address Joaquin Costa 22
28002 Madrid
Spain

Telephone +34 1 5635482
Fax +34 1 5642644

Software Micro CDS/ISIS

INTEGRATED DOCUMATICS LTD

Address Olympic House
196-200 The Broadway
Wimbledon
London SW19 1SL
UK

Telephone +44 81 543 3611
Fax +44 81 542 4415

Software OMNIDOC/IMSOFT

INTELLIGENT ARCHIVE SYSTEMS LTD

Address Fulwood House
12 Fulwood Place
London WC1V 6HR
UK

Telephone +44 71 430 2689
Fax +44 71 831 8897

Software The Corporate Retriever

INTERNATIONAL BRAINWARE

Address PO Box 423
2270 CK Voorburg
Netherlands

Telephone +31 70 3475993/3476280
Fax +31 70 3459290

Software Wordcruncher

IOTA CONSULTANCY

Address PO Box 32
7500 AA Enschede
Netherlands

Telephone +31 53 319783
Fax +31 53 301343

Software Cardbox-Plus Shell; Cardbox-Plus; BRS/Search; Picture Cardbox; Term Manager; ModiFile, the convenient converter

IRS-DIALTECH

Address The British Library
SRIS
25 Southampton Buildings
London
WC2A 1AW
UK

Telephone +44 71 323 7951/7946
Fax +44 71 323 7954

Software Mikrotel

ISL

Address 38 Rue des Etats-Généraux
78000 Versailles
France

Telephone +33 1 39 02 10 39
Fax +33 1 39 02 10 76

Software Media-Bop

JACKSON SMITH ASSOCIATES

Address 119 High Street South
Rushden
Northants NN10 0RB
UK

Telephone +44 933 311013
Fax +44 933 410750

Software RefWriter

JAN DE WINTER ADVIESBUREAU

Address PO Box 8056
1180 LB Amstelveen
Netherlands

Telephone +31 20 6438438
Fax +31 20 6438438

Software Winform

JLB INFORMATIQUE

Address 39 Boulevard Victor Hugo
92110 Clichy
France

Telephone +33 1 47 30 99 19
Fax +33 1 47 30 99 20

Software JLB DOC/JLB BIB

K. A. SPENCER

Address 74 Dovers Park
Bathford
Nr. Bath
Avon BA1 7UE
UK

Telephone +44 225 858464

Software JISYS; VISYS

KALHOST

Address Alacam Sokak No 33/4-5
Cankaya
06690 Ankara
Turkey

Telephone +90 4127 8014
Fax +90 4127 1944

Software TINlib

KARMAC BV

Address PO Box 212
8200 AE Lelystad
Netherlands

Telephone +31 3200 44244
Telex 70110 KARTO NL

Software Kambis

KING'S COLLEGE

Address Educational Comp. Unit
552 King's Road
London SW10 0UA
UK

Telephone +44 71 872 3126

Software Kermit

KNOWLEDGE SET CORPORATION

Address Suite 11
Swan Centre
Fishers Lane
London W4 1RX
UK

Telephone +44 81 995 1331
Fax +44 81 747 3640

Software HyperKRS

KOMMUNEDATA

Address Biblioteksdivisionen
Hadsundvej 194
DK-9100 Aalborg
Denmark

Software MICROMASTER

LAN SYSTEMS SRL

Address Via Roncati 9
40134 Bologna
Italy

Telephone +39 51 437 025
Fax +39 51 426 842

Software DataFlex

LANCASTER UNIVERSITY LIBRARY COMPUTING

Address Bailrigg
Lancaster
LA1 4YH
UK

Telephone +44 524 65201
Telex 65111 LANCUL G
Fax +44 524 63806

Software Lancaster University Inter-Library Loans Management System; Lanslide

LANGLET INFORMATIK

Address Hesselkaer 1
DK-7100 Vejle
Denmark

Software MikroMARC

LIB-BASE

Address The Library Office
Churchill College
Cambridge CB3 0DS
UK

Telephone +44 223 336138

Software Lib-BASE

LIBPAC COMPUTER SERVICES LTD

Address Martin House Farm
Hilltop Lane
Whittle le Woods, Chorley
Lancashire PR6 7QR
UK

Telephone +44 257 274833
Fax +44 257 266488

Software BookMarc

LIMROSE Software LTD

Address Aerial Road
Llay Industrial Estate
Wrexham
Clwyd LL12 OTU
UK

Telephone +44 978 855555

Software Progen Library

LIS

Address Prinsengracht 373
1016 HL Amsterdam
Netherlands

Telephone +31 20 252416

Software INMAGIC Plus; SearchMAGIC

LOGI+

Address 6 Rue de Stockholm
67000 Strasbourg
France

Telephone +33 88 60 17 60
Fax +33 88 61 12 72

Software GESBiB III; Bibal

LOGICAL CHOICE LTD

Address 3 Newtec Place
66-72 Magdalen Road
Oxford
OX4 1RE
UK

Telephone +44 865 200200
Fax +44 865 790853

Software Heritage

LOGITEC INFORMATICA

Address Emilio Vargas, 17
28043 Madrid
Spain

Telephone +34 1 416 4481
Fax +34 1 519 6505

Software SGBC

LOGITEC INFORMATICA

Address Cortes de Aragon, 70
50005 Zaragoza
Spain

Telephone +34 76 55 5522
Fax +34 76 35 7722

Software SGBC

MACREX INDEXING SERVICES

Address Beech House
Burn Road
Blaydon-on-Tyne
Tyne & Wear NE21 6JR
UK

Telephone +44 91 414 2595
Fax +44 91 414 2595

Software Macrex Indexing Program

MANAGEMENT SOFTWARE LTD

Address RMC House
Townmead Road
London SW6
UK

Telephone +44 71 731 7200

Software PC Anywhere

MAXOTEX

Address 66 Rue des Binelles
BP 33
92312 Sevres Cedex
Paris
France

Telephone +31 45 07 95 95

Software PC Anywhere

MCPS S.A.

Address 63 Rue du Centre
B-4800 Verviers
Belgium

Telephone +32 87 22 28 22
Fax +32 87 23 09 50

Software STAR

MECKLER LTD

Address 247-249 Vauxhall Bridge Rd
London
SW1V 1HQ
UK

Telephone +44 71 931 9985
Telex 265451 MONREF G Ref
Fax +44 71 931 8908

Software Essential Guide to Dbase IV in Libraries - On Disk

MEESTER AUTOMATISERING

Address Zesstedenweg 40
1613 KA Grootebroek
Netherlands

Telephone +31 2285 16552
Fax +31 2285 11840

Software MABB

MENTOR INFORMATIK A/S

Address Fuglevaenget 9
DK-9000 Aalborg
Denmark

Telephone +45 98 13 02 66
Fax +45 98 16 86 65

Software TINlib

MERCURY DESIGN (BURNINGBOW DIVISION)

Address 1 Mill Road
Portslade
East Sussex
BN41 1PD
UK

Telephone +44 273 412597/419989
Fax +44 273 412634

Software Libris

MFT COMPUTER SYSTEMS LTD

Address MFT House
North Parkway
Seacroft
Leeds
LS14 6PX
UK

Telephone +44 532 738244
Fax +44 532 651831

Software Records Management System

MICRO CONSULTING S.A.

Address En Budron A12
CH-1052 Le Mont
Lausanne
Switzerland

Telephone +41 21 653 2400
Fax +41 21 653 2415

Software BiblioMac

MICROCOM UK LTD

Address 2D Dukes Court
Duke Street
Woking
Surrey GU21 5BH
UK

Telephone +44 483 740763
Fax +44 483 740764

Software Carbon Copy Plus

MICRONET S.A.

Address María Tubau, 7
Edificio Auge III, 6
28049 Madrid
Spain

Telephone +34 1 372 05 17
Fax +34 1 372 05 62

Software Knosys; Clarity

MIMU'S

Address Henry Polaklaan 15 huis
Amsterdam
Netherlands

Telephone +31 20 227291

Software Octopus

DE MONTFORT UNIVERSITY LIBRARY

Address PO Box 143
Leicester
LE1 9BH
UK

Telephone +44 533 551551

Fax +44 533 550307

Software AIM-2

MORGAN BARNETT ASSOCIATES

Address Lisker House
Lisker Avenue
Otley
West Yorkshire LS21 1DG
UK

Telephone +44 943 850970

Software Phoenix Library & Resource Management System

MSC INFORMATION RETRIEVAL TECHNOLOGIES

Address Dufaystraat 1
1075 GR Amsterdam
Netherlands

Telephone +31 20 6794273
Fax +31 20 6710793

Software idealist; Zyindex; Sonar; Isys

NATIONAL DOCUMENTATION CENTRE (GREECE)

Address 48 Vas. Constantinou Ave
11635 Athens
Greece

Telephone +30 1 721 1876

Software Abekt

NEW INFORMATION PARADIGMS LTD

Address 87 Old Wokingham Road
Crowthorne
Berkshire
RG11 6LJ
UK

Telephone +44 344 778783
Fax +44 344 772510

Software The Information Partner

NEWSTAR DISTRIBUTION LTD

Address The Widford Old Rectory
London Road
Chelmsford
Essex CM2 8TE
UK

Telephone +44 245 265017
Fax +44 245 263969

Software FETCH-IT

NIC NORDIC INFO CENTER A/S

Address Bernhard Bangs Allé 23
DK-2000 Frederiksberg
Denmark

Software Mikro Polydoc

NIMO DATA AB

Address Rissneleden 138, Box 2038
172 02 Sundbyberg
Sweden

Telephone +46 8 733 2198
Fax +46 8 733 3870

Software STAR

NIVOO

Address Postbus 31262
6503 CG Nijmegen
Netherlands

Telephone +31 80 239107

Software Biblion

NORSK SENTER FOR INFORMATIKK A/S

Address PO Box 350
Blindern
0314 Oslo 3
Norway

Telephone +47 2 45 20 10

Software Mikro Polydoc

NORSK SYSTEMUTVIKLING A/S

Address Malmoe gt. 7
0566 Oslo
Norway

Telephone +47 2 37 18 00
Fax +47 2 37 07 75

Software MikroMARC; DCTS Periodicals Control System

NORTH AMERICAN SOFTWARE GMBH

Address Uhde Strasse 40
8000 Munich 71
Germany

Telephone +49 89 791 7091

Software askSam

OCLC EUROPE

Address 7th Floor, Tricorn House
51-53 Hagley Road
Birmingham
B16 8TP
UK

Telephone +44 21 456 4656
Telex 335176 OCLC TFSTRS G
Fax +44 21 456 4680

Software OCLC Cataloguing Software

ODIS

Address Ninoofsesteenweg 244
B-1700 Dilbeek
Belgium

Telephone +32 2 569 66 96
Fax +32 2 569 80 72

Software VUBIS

ODIS FRANCE

Address Les Trois Fontaines
BP 1004
95000 Cergy
France

Software VUBIS

ODIS PAYS-BAS

Address Piazza 403
5611 AG Eindhoven
Netherlands

Software Vubis

OMEGON COMPUTERSYSTEMEN BV

Address PO Box 755
3900 AT Veenendaal
Netherlands

Telephone +31 8385 40404

Software STAR

OPSYS

Address 3 Rue Paul Valérien Perrin
38170 Seyssinet-Pariset
France

Telephone +33 76 49 04 40
Fax +33 76 48 35 00

Software OPSYS

ORACLE CORPORATION UK LTD

Address Oracle Centre
The Ring
Bracknell
Berkshire RG12 1BW
UK

Telephone +44 344 860066
Fax +44 344 860222

Software Oracle Libraries

ORMAS AUTOMATISERING

Address Elzenkade 1
3992 AD Houten
Netherlands

Telephone +31 3403 90911

Software Bibliotheek en Documentatie Pakket (BGD-Pakket)

OVM SOPIANA

Address Progress House
301-303 Mitcham Road
London SW17 9JQ
UK

Telephone +44 81 672 6537

Software Gofer; Sidetalk

OXFORD UNIVERSITY PRESS

Address Walton Street
Oxford
OX2 6DP
UK

Telephone +44 865 267979
Telex 837330 OXPRESS
Fax +44 865 56646

Software Micro-OCP

OY OPEN SOFTWARE SOLUTIONS AB

Address Bankgatan 6
66900 Nykarleby
Finland

Telephone +358 (9)67 221 111
Fax +358 (9)67 221 550

Software GEMINI

P.M. VAN VELSEN / A. KNEVEL

Address Rembrandtlaan 88
2271 GK Voorburg
Netherlands

Telephone +31 79 517644

Software V-K uitleensysteem

P&P MICRO DISTRIBUTORS LTD

Address 1 Gleneagle Road
London
SW16 6AW
UK

Telephone +44 81 677 8155
Telex 919220 PPMICR G
Fax +44 81 677 4335

Software SMARTERM

P&P MICRO DISTRIBUTORS LTD

Address 9th Floor
1 Victoria Square
Birmingham
B1 1BN
UK

Telephone +44 21 643 2121
Telex 265871 MONREF G

Software SMARTERM

P&P MICRO DISTRIBUTORS LTD

Address Todd Hall Road
Carrs Industrial Estate
Haslingden
Rossendale
Lancashire BB4 5HU
UK

Telephone +44 706 211744
Telex 635740 PPMICR G
Fax +44 706 211401

Software SMARTERM

PC COMMUNICATIONS LTD

Address Elmsdale House
31 The Green
West Drayton
Middlesex UB7 7PN
UK

Telephone +44 895 444455
Telex 926119 PCC G
Fax +44 895 444452

Software Breakout Plus; Mass Breakout

PC SECURITY

Address Gerner-Mathisen Garden
Elueveien 25 B
PO Box 109
1324 Lysaker
Norway

Telephone +47 2 53 1153

Software PC Anywhere

PERSONAL BIBLIOGRAPHIC SOFTWARE

Address Woodside
Hinksey Hill
Oxford OX1 5AU
UK

Telephone +44 865 730275
Fax +44 865 736354

Software Biblio-Link; Pro-Cite; Pro-Search

PHOTOBASE LTD

Address Trafalgar House
Grenville Place
Mill Hill
London NW7 3SA
UK

Telephone +44 81 959 4060
Fax +44 81 959 3605

Software Livelink

PHOTOFILE LTD

Address Unit 5, 110 Coast Road
West Mersea
Colchester
Essex CO5 8PA
UK

Telephone +44 206 385249
Fax +44 206 385315

Software Phototracer

PICA

Address PO Box 876
2300 AW Leiden
Netherlands

Telephone +31 71 257257
Fax +31 71 223119

Software Micro-OPC

PLATINUM S.A.

Address Parc des Barbanniers 1
Place des Hauts-Tilliers
92632 Gennevilliers Cedex
France

Telephone +33 1 46 85 24 24
Fax +33 1 47 98 28 38

Software Biblio-Tech; Documenta; CoLibris

POLYPHOT

Address 72 Quai des Carrières
94220 Charenton le Pont
Paris
France

Telephone +33 1 49 77 08 20
Fax +33 1 49 77 04 36

Software POLYBASE/DIDEROT

POLYPHOT (UK) LTD

Address 56 Queens Gate Terrace
London
SW7 5PJ
UK

Telephone +44 71 636 0440/584 2935
Fax +44 71 240 1891

Software POLYBASE/DIDEROT

PORTSMOUTH POLYTECHNIC

Address Frewen Library
Cambridge Road
Portsmouth PO1 2ST
UK

Telephone +44 705 843236
Fax +44 705 843233

Software MILL-IV

PRETTYBIT SOFTWARES

Address Yliopistonkatu 58-60 B
33100 Tampere
Finland

Software PRETTYLIB

QCL SOLUTIONS

Address Stubbins Lane
Stubbins
Ramsbottom
Lancashire BL0 0NH
UK

Telephone +44 706 827811
Fax +44 706 822697

Software Equilibrium

RELAIS INFORMATIQUE INTERNATIONAL

Address 7 Rue Charles Dordain BP 74
93600 Aulnay-sous-Bois
Cedex
France

Telephone +33 1 48 79 07 02
Fax +33 1 48 79 39 75

Software LIBER

RELAY COMMUNICATIONS UK

Address 2B Dukes Court
Dukes Street
Woking
Surrey GU21 5BH
UK

Telephone +44 483 740763

Software Carbon Copy Plus

RICHARD CUMMING AND ASSOCIATES

Address Springfield House
Witney Street
Burford
Oxon
OX18 4DR
UK

Telephone +44 993 823737
Fax +44 993 823784

Software Multicom

RISC DEVELOPMENTS LTD

Address 117 Hatfield Road
St Albans
Herts
AL1 4JS
UK

Telephone +44 727 40303
Fax +44 727 860263

Software Masterfile II/III

RIVA LTD

Address 3 Bentley Industrial Estate
Bentley
Farnham
GU10 5NJ
UK

Telephone +44 420 22666
Telex 9312100402
Fax +44 420 23700

Software Gofer

ROBERT FOX AND ASSOCIATES

Address 27 Harlestone Close
Luton
Bedfordshire LU3 4DW
UK

Telephone +44 582 572 148

Software Amitel

ROLA HARD- UND SOFTWAREBERATUNG GMBH

Address Thunstrasse 9
CH-3700 Speiz
Switzerland

Telephone +41 33 54 80 44
Fax +41 33 54 86 44

Software TINlib

ROYAL SCHOOL OF LIBRARIANSHIP

Address Birketinget 6
DK-2300 Copenhagen
Denmark

Telephone +45 31 58 60 66
Fax +45 32 84 02 01

Software Micro CDS/ISIS; MicroBES

ROYAL SOCIETY OF CHEMISTRY

Address Thomas Graham House
Science Park
Milton Road
Cambridge CB4 4WF
UK

Telephone +44 223 420066
Telex 818293 ROYAL
Fax +44 223 423623

Software STN Express

RUBBER CONSULTANTS

Address Brickendonbury
Hertford
Hertfordshire
SG13 8NL
UK

Telephone +44 992 554657
Telex G817449 MRRBDL

Software MORPHS

S B ELECTRONIC SYSTEMS LTD

Address Arden Grove
Harpenden
Hertfordshire
AL5 4SL
UK

Telephone +44 582 769991
Telex 82350
Fax +44 582 461705

Software Telepen Library System

S.E.I. (IGNACIO MEGIAS)

Address C/Zurbano 41
28001 Madrid
Spain

Telephone +34 1 419 2208
Fax +34 1 419 8673

Software DataFlex

THE SAGE GROUP PLC

Address Sage House
Benton Park Road
Newcastle upon Tyne
NE7 7LZ
UK

Telephone +44 91 201 3000
Fax +44 91 201 0308

Software Chit-Chat

SAMSOM-VELDKAMP

Address Wibautstraat 129
1091 GL Amsterdam
Netherlands

Telephone +31 20 6683191

Software STRIDE

SERVICIOS AUXILIARES LINGUISTICOS

Address Andres Mellado, 9 (1-D)
28015 Madrid
Spain

Software Biblio-Tech

SERVICIOS DE TELEDOCUMENTACION, S.A.

Address Luchana no. 4, 2. A-B
28010 Madrid
Spain

Telephone +34 1 593 96 12
Fax +34 1 593 98 21

Software ABSYS

SHAREWARE MARKETING

Address 3a Queen Street
Seaton
Devon
EX12 2NY
UK

Telephone +44 297 24088
Fax +44 297 24091

Software Memory Mate; ProComm Plus; Odyssey

SILVERPLATTER INFORMATION LTD

Address 10 Barley Mow Passage
Chiswick
London W4 4PH
UK

Telephone +44 81 995 8242

Software Reference Manager

SIMS LTD

Address The SIMS Centre
Abbot's Road
Priory Business Park
Cardington
Bedford
MK44 3SG
UK

Telephone +44 234 838080
Fax +44 234 838091

Software SIMS Library Management Module

SINORG

Address Département Administration
12 rue Rouget de l'Isle
Aix Seine 20
92442 Issy le Moulineux
Paris
France

Telephone +33 1 46 62 30 00
Fax +33 1 46 62 32 27

Software BRS/Search

SIRSI LTD

Address Suite A, Deneway House
Darkes Lane
Potters Bar
Hertfordshire EN6 1AQ
UK

Telephone +44 707 47039
Fax +44 707 47517

Software Unicorn Collection Management System

SISMACRO

Address Ave Miguel Bombarda 147
1000 Lisbon
Portugal

Telephone +351 1 3528521

Software Knosys; Clarity

SMALLSOFT

Address PO Box 68
Loughborough
Leicestershire LE11 OFX
UK

Telephone +44 509 880059
Fax +44 509 880059

Software Communicator

SOFT OPTIONS (COMPUTER SYSTEMS) LTD

Address Dean Clough Industrial Park
Halifax
West Yorkshire HX3 5AR
UK

Telephone +44 422 330428
Fax +44 422 368612

Software Folio Views

SOFTKEY

Address Gedempte Gracht 4
Deventer
Netherlands

Telephone +31 5700 11313

Software Microsoft-ACCESS; CROSSTALK XVI; Relay Gold; ZyIndex

SOFTKLONE (UK) LTD

Address Preview House
Boundary Road
Loudwater
High Wycombe
Buckinghamshire HP10 9QT
UK

Telephone +44 628 819200
Fax +44 628 810314

Software MIRROR III

SOFTLINK EUROPE LTD

Address 1 Thorncliffe Road
Oxford OX2 7BA
UK

Telephone +44 865 311902/511175
Fax +44 865 311115

Software Alice

THE Software HOUSE

Address Claridge House
29 Barnes High Street
London
SE13 9LW
UK

Telephone +44 81 876 8660

Software INFOLINK

Software SOLUTIONS

Address 70-72 St Marks Road
Maidenhead
Berkshire SL6 6DW
UK

Telephone +44 628 781135/770002
Fax +44 628 73177

Software EXTRACT

SOUTHDATA LTD

Address Voysey House
Barley Mow Passage
London W4 4PT
UK

Telephone +44 71 995 7587/7967/9188
Fax +44 71 994 4959

Software Athene; Colossus; Convert; Superfile

SOUTRON LTD

Address Jerome House
Hallam Fields Road
Ilkeston
Derbyshire DE7 4BH
UK

Telephone +44 602 441664
Fax +44 602 441626

Software Soutron Library System; INMAGIC Plus; SearchMAGIC; INMAGIC Image; MARC Adaptor; MULTI Adaptor

SQUARE BV

Address Buitenop 5
6041 LA Roermond
Netherlands

Telephone +31 4750 34999
Fax +31 4750 11675

Software BIBIS

STICHTING VRIENDEN VAN ARCHIEF EN LIBRIJE

Address PO Box 454
2800 AL Gouda
Netherlands

Telephone +31 1820 16135

Software askSam

STN INTERNATIONAL

Address PO Box 2465
7500 Karlsruhe 1
Germany

Telephone +49 7247 808 555
Telex 17724710
Fax +49 7247 808 666

Software STN Express

STN INTERNATIONAL

Address c/o FIZ Karlsruhe
PO Box 2465
7500 Karlsruhe
Germany

Telephone +49 7247 808 555
Telex 17724710
Fax +49 7247 808 666

Software STN Personal File System; STN Express

SWEETENS COMPUTER SERVICES

Address 7 Fishergate Court
Preston
Lancashire PR1 8QF
UK

Telephone +44 772 52443
Fax +44 772 561012

Software STAR

SWETS UK LTD

Address 32 Blacklands Way
Abingdon Business Park
Abingdon
Oxfordshire OX14 1SX

Telephone +44 235 530809
Fax +44 235 535055

Software SAILS

SWETS & ZEITLINGER BV

Address Heereweg 347b
2161 CA Lisse
Netherlands

Telephone +31 2521 35111
Fax +31 2521 15888

Software SAILS

SWISSTAR SOFTWARE

Address PO Box 2965
3000 CZ Rotterdam
Netherlands

Telephone +31 10 4333170

Software RAIZ; SWISSTAR

SWS SOFTWARE SYSTEMS AG

Address Postfach
CH-3172 Niederwangen
Switzerland

Telephone +41 31 34 32 63
Fax +41 31 34 06 66

Software BIBLIO; Micro-VTLS

SYNAPS AUTOMATISERING BV

Address PO Box 56
8325 ZH Vollenhove
Netherlands

Telephone +31 5274 3535

Software ADIOS

SYS-DIS

Address Le Clemenceau 1
205 Ave Georges Clemenceau
92000 Nanterre Cedex
France

Telephone +33 1 47 24 19 61
Fax +33 1 47 24 15 76

Software DataFlex

SYSTEMATIC UPGRADE COMPUTER CONSULTANTS LTD

Address 58-60 Edward Road
New Barnet
Hertfordshire EN4 8A7
UK

Telephone +44 81 449 9699
Fax +44 81 441 2297

Software Personal Librarian

TAMIL

Address 91 Bd Edmond Rostand
92500 Rueil-Malmaison
France

Telephone +33 1 47 32 35 34
Telex 270105F txfra/ref 345

Software TAMIL

TELESYSTÈMES QUESTEL

Address 83-85 Boulevard Vincent Auriol
75013 Paris
France

Telephone +33 1 45 82 64 64
Telex 204594F
Fax +33 1 45 85 43 08

Software Micro-Questel; DARC-CHEMLINK

TELESYSTEMS LTD

Address 3 Wycombe Road
Prestwood
Buckinghamshire
HP16 0ND
UK

Telephone +44 2406 6365
Fax +44 2406 6365

Software PC Anywhere; ASCOM IV; Reachout

TEXT AND VIDEO SYSTEMS LTD

Address 4 Fawley Road
London NW6 1SH
UK

Telephone +44 71 435 2060
Fax +44 81 343 2461

Software VTEXT

TH-DATA OY

Address 69600 Kaustinen
Finland

Software FINTEK

TITE-LIVE S.A.

Address Rue de la borgnette 15
B-7500 Tournai
Belgium

Software BIBULUS; DEBORA-DOC

TOP-TECH-SYSTEMS

Address 33 Caernarvon Road
Norwich
Norfolk NR2 3HZ
UK

Telephone +44 603 617684

Software Micro-Library-System (MLS)

TOPIS INTERNATIONAL

Address Rua Prof. Jorge Miniero
Lote 44, Loja 9
Queluz DeBaxio
Portugal

Telephone +351 1 955 452
Fax +351 1 956 405

Software DataFlex

TRANSACTION POINT LTD

Address Stuart House
43/47 Crown Street
Reading
Berkshire RG1 2SN
UK

Telephone +44 734 866276

Software File Registry System

UNESCO

Address XLAD/UNESCO
7 Place de Fontenoy
75007 Paris
France

Telephone +33 1 45 68 10 00
Telex 204461
Fax +33 1 43 06 16 40

Software Micro CDS/ISIS

UNESCO CENTRUM NEDERLAND

Address Oranjestraat 10
2514 JB Den Haag
Netherlands

Telephone +31 70 3644655

Software Micro CDS/ISIS

UNILÓGICA

Address Rua D. Nuno Alvares Pereira
52-A
2330 Entroncamento
Portugal

Telephone +351 49 71 77 17
Fax +351 49 71 81 94

Software TINlib

UNINA S.A.

Address Rue de Coquelet 134
B-5000 Namur
Belgium

Telephone +32 81 23 11 10
Telex 59320 B
Fax +32 81 22 40 00

Software PCTEX

UNISYS ESPAÑA S.A.

Address Martinez Villergas 1
Edificio Unisys
28027 Madrid
Spain

Telephone +34 1 403 6000/405 3011
Fax +34 1 403 6461

Software TINlib

UNIVERSITÉ CATHOLIQUE DE LOUVAIN

Address Bibliothèque des Sciences Economiques, Sociales et Politiques
Place Montesquieu 1. B.te 18
B-1348 Louvain-La-Neuve
Belgium

Telephone +32 10 47 42 69
Fax +32 10 47 42 67

Software Micro CDS/ISIS

VICOM LTD

Address 34-36 Poole Road
Bournemouth
Dorset
BH2 5PT
UK

Telephone +44 202 293233
Fax +44 202 310241

Software VICOM

VTLS INC.

Address Hewlett Packard Española S.A.
Avda. Diagonal, 605
08028 Barcelona
Spain

Telephone +34 3 401 91 63
Fax +34 3 430 84 68

Software Micro-VTLS

VTLS OF FINLAND OY

Address Teollisuuskatu 23-25
SF 00510 Helsinki
Finland

Telephone +358 0 701 3047
Fax +358 0 701 3173

Software Micro-VTLS

WENNERGREN-WILLIAMS INFORMATIONSSOKNUNG AB

Address PO Box 30004
104 25 Stockholm
Sweden

Telephone +46 8 54 1200

Software INFOLINK

WIGHT SCIENTIFIC

Address 44 Roan Street
London
SE10 9JT
UK

Telephone +44 81 858 2699
Fax +44 81 853 4416

Software PAPERbase De Luxe

WINCH SRL

Address Via Euripide 1
20145 Milano
Italy

Telephone +39 2 4800 6009
Fax +39 2 4814 736

Software HEADFAST;
HEADFAST/CD;
HEADFORM;
HEADLINE; HEADSET

WOLTERS KLUWER DSS BV

Address PO Box 362
2400 AJ Alphen aan den Rijn
Netherlands

Telephone +31 720 62650/90150
Fax +31 720 62692

Software Infodown; Infolog;
Infotrans; Mikro Polydoc

X-ON Software LTD

Address 65 Victoria Road
London N22 4XA
UK

Telephone +44 81 881 3659

Software CONTACT

Z A G COMPUTING

Address Agerbaekvej 6
DK-2650 Hvidovre
Denmark

Software MicroFind

Function Index

FUNCTION INDEX

BIBIS
Biblio-Plus
Biblio-Tech
BiblioMac
Bibliotheek en Documentatie
Pakket (BGD - Pakket)
Biblix
Bido
BIS-LOK
BookMarc
CAIRS LMS
CALM
CIBIS (Cipal Bibliotheek Systeem)
CLASS
Data Trek
DIVA
Dynix
ELROND
Equilibrium
GEMINI
GIBUS
HEADFAST
Heritage
Influx
Infokraft Library System
INMAGIC Plus
JLB DOC/JLB BIB
KAMBIS
Lanslide
Lexicon
Lib-BASE
LIBER
LIBMAN
LIBRARIAN
LIBRARY 2000
LibraryPac 1
LibraryPac 2/LibraryPac 3
LIBRI
Libris
LICON
Logabib
MABB
Mac School Library
MDUP
Media-Bop
Micro-Library-System (MLS)
Micro-OPC
Micro-VTLS
MikroMARC
OASIS
OCLC Cataloguing Software
Octopus
OPSYS
Oracle Libraries
Paprika
Phoenix Library & Resource
Management System
POLYBASE/DIDEROT
Progen Library
SABINI
SGBC
SIMS Library Management Module
Soutron Library System
TAMIL
THOT
TINinc
TINlib
TINphoto
Unicorn Collection Management
System
Vubis
Winform

CD-ROM INTERFACE

Full/Text
HEADFAST
HEADFAST/CD
SearchMAGIC
TINlib

CHEMICAL INFORMATION

- DARC-CHEMLINK
- STN EXPRESS

CIRCULATION

- ABSYS
- ADLIB Lite
- Afibyblos
- Aleph/PC
- Alexandrie II
- Alice
- Analogio
- Artemis
- ATBiB
- Babylone Documentation
- Bibal
- BIBIS
- BiblioMac
- Biblio-Plus
- Biblio-Tech
- Biblix
- BIS-LOK
- CAIRS LMS
- CALM
- CIBIS (Cipal Bibliotheek Systeem)
- CLASS
- Data Trek
- ELROND
- Equilibrium
- GEMINI
- GIBUS
- HEADFAST
- Heritage
- Influx
- Infokraft Library System
- INMAGIC Plus
- JLB DOC/JLB BIB
- KAMBIS
- Lexicon
- Lib-BASE
- LIBMAN
- LIBRARIAN
- LIBRARY 2000
- LibraryPac 2/LibraryPac 3
- LIBRI
- Libris
- LICON
- Logabib
- MABB
- Mac School Library
- Media-Bop
- Micro-Library-System (MLS)
- Micro-VTLS
- MikroMARC
- OASIS
- OPSYS
- Oracle Libraries
- Paprika
- Phoenix Library & Resource Management System
- POLYBASE/DIDEROT
- Progen Library
- SABINI
- SGBC
- SIMS Library Management Module
- Soutron Library System
- TAMIL
- Telepen Library System
- TINlib
- Unicorn Collection Management System
- V-K uitleensysteem
- Vubis
- Winform

COMMUNICATIONS

- ACOM
- Amitel
- ASCOM IV
- Basil

EndNote
FILTER
HEADFORM
INFODOWN
The Information Partner
LITREF
MARC Adaptor
ModiFile, the convenient converter
MULTI Adaptor
RAIZ
RefWriter
SWISSTAR
Synopsys
TINlib

DATABASE MANAGEMENT

DataFlex
Folio Views
LOGOTEX
MASTERFILE II/III
STAR

DOWNLOADING

ACOM
BiB/SEARCH
BLAISE Recorder
Chit-Chat
CONTACT
CROSSTALK XVI
Datatalk
DIALOGLINK
HEADLINE
I&D Software
INFOLINK
INFOLOG
The Information Partner
Mass Breakout
Micro-Questel
Mikrotel
Odyssey
PCTEX
Pro-Search
ProComm Plus
Relay Gold
SALBIN PC
SMARTCOM II
SMARTERM
Supercom
VICOM
XMODEM PC

ELECTRONIC MAIL

Chit-Chat
CONTACT
Datatalk
Infolink
Multicom

FILE INDEXING

GOfer
Isys
Recall Plus
Sonar
ZyIndex

FREE TEXT RETRIEVAL

The Corporate Retriever
EXTRACT
FreeForm
Recall Plus
Status/PC
Textmaster
Topic

GRAPHICAL USER INTERFACE

Cardbox-Plus Shell

GRAPHICS

I&D Software

GESBiB III
HEADFAST
HEADFAST/CD
ideaList
Influx
INMAGIC Plus
Isys
JISYS
JLB DOC/JLB BIB
KAWare
Knosys
Knowledgebase
LibraryPac 1
LibraryPac 2/LibraryPac 3
LITREF
LOGOTEX
MABB
Memolog 2
Memory Mate
Micro CDS/ISIS
Micro-Questel
Mikro Polydoc
MikroMARC
MORPHS
OASIS
OpAcc
ORIEL
PAPERbase De Luxe
PC Master
PC Stairs
Personal Librarian
Phototracer
Picture Cardbox
Pro-Cite
QUEST
RASMUS
Recall Plus
Reference Manager
Refsys Super
SABINI
SearchMAGIC
Sonar
STAR
Status/PC
STN Personal File System
Strix
SUPERDOC
Superfile
TAMIL
Texplore
Textmaster
TEXTO
TINinc
TINphoto
Topic
VISYS
VTEXT
ZyIndex

INTEGRATED LIBRARY HOUSEKEEPING

ABSYS
ADLIB Lite
Afibyblos
Aleph/PC
Alice
Analogio
Bibal
BIBIS
Biblio-Tech
Biblix
BIS-LOK
CAIRS LMS
CALM
CIBIS (Cipal Bibliotheek Systeem)
Data Trek
Dynix
Equilibrium
GEMINI
Heritage

I&D Software
INFOLINK
Infolink
INFOLOG
Mass Breakout
Micro-Questel
Mikrotel
MIRROR III
Multicom
Odyssey
Pro-Search
ProComm Plus
Sherlock
Sidetalk
SMARTCOM II
STN EXPRESS
XMODEM PC

OPAC

ABSYS
ADLIB Lite
Alice
BiblioMac
BIS-LOK
CAIRS LMS
CIBIS (Cipal Bibliotheek Systeem)
Dynix
Equilibrium
GEMINI
GIBUS
HEADFAST
Lexicon
LIBER
LIBMAN
LIBRARIAN
Micro-OPC
Micro-VTLS
MikroMARC
OASIS
OPSYS
Oracle Libraries
POLYBASE/DIDEROT
SearchMAGIC
Soutron Library System
THOT
TINlib
Unicorn Collection Management System
Vubis

PERSONAL BIBLIOGRAPHIC DATABASE

AutoBiblio
BiB/SEARCH
Biblion
Cardbox-Plus
Documenta
EndNote
ideaList
JISYS
LITREF
Micro CDS/ISIS
PAPERbase De Luxe
Pro-Cite
RASMUS
Reference Manager
Refsys Super
STN Personal File System
VISYS

RECORDS MANAGEMENT

CORA
File Registry System
OMNIDOC/IMSOFT
Records Management System

REFERENCE MANAGEMENT

AutoBiblio
BiB/SEARCH
Biblion

Operating Systems Index

OPERATING SYSTEMS INDEX

Logabib
LOGOTEX
MABB
Macrex Indexing Program
MagicKey
MARC Adaptor
Mass Breakout
MDUP
Memolog 2
Memory Mate
Micro CDS/ISIS
Micro-Library-System (MLS)
Micro-OCP
Micro-OPC
Micro-Questel
Micro-VTLS
MicroLinx
Microsoft-ACCESS
Mikro Polydoc
MikroMARC
Mikrotel
MILL-IV
MIRROR III
ModiFile, the convenient converter
MORPHS
MULTI Adaptor
Multicom
OASIS
OASIS-AIM
OASIS-SMS
OCLC Cataloguing Software
Octopus
Odyssey
OMNIDOC/IMSOFT
ONLINE SEARCH TUTOR
JUNIOR (OST Junior)
OORNINKI
OpAcc
PAPERbase De Luxe
Paprika
PATCHWORK
PC Anywhere
PC Master
PC-Order/PC-Order Plus/PC-Query
PC Stairs
PCTEX
Personal Librarian
Phototracer
Picture Cardbox
Picture Frame
POLYBASE/DIDEROT
PRETTYLIB
Pro-Cite
Pro-Search
ProComm Plus
Progen Library
q-CAL
QUEST
RAIZ
RASMUS
Reachout
Recall Plus
Reference Manager
Refsys Super
RefWriter
Relay Gold
SAILS
SALBIN PC
SearchMAGIC
SGBC
Sherlock
Sidetalk
SIMS Library Management Module
SMARTCOM II
SMARTCOM III
SMARTERM
SOD
Soutron Library System
Status/PC
STN EXPRESS

SABINI
THOT

RISC OS (ARCHIMEDES)

JISYS
MASTERFILE II/III
QUEST
VISYS

UNIX

ABSYS
ADIOS
Aleph/PC
BiB/SEARCH
BIBIS
Bibliotheek en Documentatie Pakket (BGD - Pakket)
Bido
BIS-LOK
BRS/Search
CAIRS IMS
CAIRS LMS
CIBIS (Cipal Bibliotheek Systeem)
Convert
The Corporate Retriever
DataFlex
DCTS Periodicals Control System
DV-ONE
Dynix
Equilibrium
EXTRACT
GEMINI
I&D Software
Influx
INFOLINK
JLB DOC/JLB BIB
Lexicon
LIBER
LIBMAN
LIBRARY 2000
Logabib
LOGOTEX
Media-Bop
OMNIDOC/IMSOFT
OpAcc
OPSYS
Oracle Libraries
Personal Librarian
POLYBASE/DIDEROT
Records Management System
SABINI
Soutron Library System
STAR
STRIDE
Strix
Superfile
Syllabus
TAMIL
TEXTO
THOT
TINinc
TINlib
TINphoto
Topic
Unicorn Collection Management System
Vubis
ZyIndex

Geographical Index

GEOGRAPHICAL INDEX

UK

Term Manager
Texplore
Textmaster
TINlib
TMS
Topic
Unicorn Collection Management
System
VICOM
VISYS
VTEXT